Women, Peace and Security

Study submitted by the Secretary-General pursuant to
Security Council resolution 1325 (2000)

United Nations
2002

NOTE

The designations employed and the presentation of the material in this publication do not imply the expression of any opinion whatsoever on the part of the Secretariat of the United Nations concerning the legal status of any country, territory, city or area or of its authorities, or concerning the delimitation of its frontiers or boundaries. The term "country" as used in the text of this publication also refers, as appropriate, to territories or areas.

Symbols of United Nations documents are composed of capital letters combined with figures.

United Nations Publication

Sales No.E.03.IV.1

ISBN 92-1-130222-6

Contents

Abbreviations vii

Foreword xi

Acknowledgements xiii

   I.   Introduction 1

  II. Impact of Armed Conflict on Women and Girls 13
       A. Violence against women and girls 14
       B. Health of women and girls 18
       C. Socio-economic dimensions 22
       D. Displacement: women and girls as refugees, returnees
           and internally displaced persons 25
       E. Disappearance and detention 29
       F. Challenges to gender roles and relations 30

 III. International Legal Framework 33
       A. International humanitarian law and human rights law .. 33
       B. Redress for women and girls for conflict-related
           abuses 38
       C. Reparations for victims of conflict 46
       D. Protecting refugee and internally displaced women
           and girls 47
       E. Challenges 48

 IV. Peace Processes 53
       A. Involvement of women and girls in informal peace
           processes 53
       B. Involvement of women and girls in formal peace
           processes 58
       C. Responses and challenges 66

V.   Peacekeeping Operations   73
      A. Gender perspectives in peace operations   74
      B. Responses and challenges   79

VI.   Humanitarian Operations   93
      A. Gender perspectives in humanitarian operations   94
      B. Responses and challenges ....…..........   98

VII. Reconstruction and Rehabilitation   111
      A. Political, civil and judicial reconstruction   111
      B. Economic reconstruction   115
      C. Social reconstruction ....…...   118
      D. Responses and challenges   122

VIII. Disarmament, Demobilization and Reintegration   129
      A. Disarmament   130
      B. Demobilization   131
      C. Reintegration   134

Notes ....….....   139

Annex – Security Council resolution 1325 (2000)   165

Bibliography   169

Abbreviations

AU	African Union (formerly Organization of African Unity)
BONUCA	United Nations Peace-building Support Mission in the Central African Republic
CAP	Consolidated Appeals Process
CARE	Cooperative for Assistance and Relief Everywhere
CEDAW	Convention on the Elimination of All Forms of Discrimination against Women
CVA	Capacities and Vulnerabilities Analysis
DAW	Division for the Advancement of Women
DDA	Department for Disarmament Affairs
DDR	Disarmament, demobilization and reintegration
DESA	Department of Economic and Social Affairs
DFAIT	Canadian Department of Foreign Affairs and International Trade
DFID	United Kingdom Department for International Development
DPA	Department of Political Affairs
DPI	Department of Public Information
DPKO	Department of Peacekeeping Operations
ECA	Economic Commission for Africa
ECHA	Executive Committee on Humanitarian Affairs
ECOWAS	Economic Community of West African States
FAO	Food and Agriculture Organization of the United Nations
FMLN	Farabundo Marti National Liberation (El Salvador)
HIV/AIDS	Human immunodeficiency virus/acquired immunodeficiency syndrome
IASC	Inter-Agency Standing Committee
ICC	International Criminal Court
ICRC	International Committee of the Red Cross

ICTR	International Criminal Tribunal for Rwanda
ICTY	International Criminal Tribunal for the former Yugoslavia
IDP	Internally displaced person
IFP	InFocus Programme
IFRC	International Federation of Red Cross and Red Crescent Societies
ILO	International Labour Organization
IOM	International Organization for Migration
MONUC	United Nations Mission in the Democratic Republic of the Congo
NATO	North Atlantic Treaty Organization
NGO	Non-governmental organization
OAS	Organization of American States
OAU	Organization for African Unity
OCHA	Office for the Coordination of Humanitarian Affairs
OHCHR	Office of the High Commissioner for Human Rights
OHRM	Office of Human Resources Management
OSAGI	Office of the Special Adviser on Gender Issues and Advancement of Women
OSCE	Organization for Security and Co-operation in Europe
OSRSG/CAC	Office of the Special Representative of the Secretary-General for Children and Armed Conflict
OXFAM	Oxford Committee for Famine Relief
SOP	Standard Operating Procedure
SRSG	Special Representative of the Secretary-General
STI	Sexually transmitted infection
STOP	Special Trafficking Operations Programme
TES	Training and Evaluation Service
UNAMA	United Nations Assistance Mission in Afghanistan
UNAMSIL	United Nations Assistance Mission in Sierra Leone
UNAVEM II	United Nations Angola Verification Mission II

UNDAF	United Nations Development Assistance Framework
UNDP	United Nations Development Programme
UNESCO	United Nations Educational, Scientific and Cultural Organization
UNIFIL	United Nations Interim Force in Lebanon
UNFPA	United Nations Population Fund
UNHCR	United Nations High Commissioner for Refugees
UNICEF	United Nations Children's Fund
UNIFEM	United Nations Development Fund for Women
UNITAR	United Nations Institute for Training and Research
UNMEE	United Nations Missions in Ethiopia and Eritrea
UNMIBH	United Nations Mission to Bosnia and Herzegovina
UNMIK	United Nations Mission in Kosovo
UNMOGIP	United Nations Military Observer Group in India and Pakistan
UNOGBIS	United Nations Peace-building Support Office in Guinea-Bissau
UNOL	United Nations Peace-building Support Office in Liberia
UNOMIG	United Nations Observer Mission in Georgia
UNTAC	United Nations Transitional Authority in Cambodia
UNTAET	United Nations Transitional Administration in East Timor
UNTOP	United Nations Tajikistan Office of Peace-building
UNU	United Nations University
WFP	World Food Programme
WHO	World Health Organization
WILPF	Women's International League for Peace and Freedom

THE SECRETARY-GENERAL

FOREWORD TO THE STUDY ON WOMEN, PEACE AND SECURITY

Most of today's conflicts take place within states. Their root causes often include poverty, the struggle for scarce resources, and violations of human rights. They have another tragic feature in common: women and girls suffer their impact disproportionately. While women and girls endure the same trauma as the rest of the population -- bombings, famines, epidemics, mass executions, torture, arbitrary imprisonment, forced migration, ethnic cleansing, threats and intimidation -- they are also targets of specific forms of violence and abuse, including sexual violence and exploitation.

Efforts to resolve these conflicts and address their root causes will not succeed unless we empower all those who have suffered from them -- including and especially women. Only if women play a full and equal part can we build the foundations for enduring peace -- development, good governance, human rights and justice.

In conflict areas across the world, women's movements have worked with the United Nations to rebuild the structures of peace and security, to rehabilitate and reconcile societies, to protect refugees and the internally displaced, to educate and raise awareness of human rights and the rule of law. Within the Organization itself, the integration of gender perspectives in peace and security areas has become a central strategy. An Inter-agency Task Force on Women, Peace and Security has been established to address the role of women in peacemaking, peacekeeping, humanitarian assistance and other activities.

This study, like the Inter-agency Task Force, is an initiative undertaken in response to Security Council resolution 1325 on women, peace and security adopted in October 2000 – in which the Council underlined the vital role of women in conflict solution, and mandated a review of the impact of armed conflict on women and girls, the role of women in peacebuilding, and the gender dimensions of peace processes and conflict resolution.

While the study shows that many positive steps have been taken to implement the resolution, women still form a minority of those who participate in peace and security negotiations, and receive less attention than men in post-conflict agreements, disarmament and reconstruction. Our challenge remains the full implementation of the landmark document that resolution 1325 represents. This study points the way to a more systematic way forward.

Kofi A. Annan

Acknowledgements

The study was prepared within the framework of the Inter-agency Task Force on Women, Peace and Security and coordinated by the Special Adviser of the Secretary-General on Gender Issues and Advancement of Women. Task Force members developed the outline of the study, provided input from headquarter and field perspectives, commented on several drafts and provided input to the formulation of recommendations.

The Task Force included representatives from the following United Nations departments, funds, programmes, funds and specialized agencies (in alphabetical order): DDA, DESA/DAW, DPA, DPI, DPKO, ILO, OCHA, OHCHR, OHRM, OSAGI, OSRSG/CAC, UNDP, UNFPA, UNHCR, UNICEF, UNIFEM, UNU and WFP. Observers included the International Committee of the Red Cross (ICRC), the International Organization for Migration (IOM) and the NGO Working Group for Women, Peace and Security (Hague Appeal for Peace, International Alert, International Women's Tribune Center, Women's Caucus for Gender Justice, Women's Commission on Refugee Women and Children and Women's International League for Peace and Freedom).

In order to ensure that the study would reflect a balanced range of experiences, and would draw on as many regional perspectives as possible, a Review Group was established to provide additional inputs and to review drafts of the study. The Review Group consisted of experienced practitioners from different conflict areas and experts in policy and legal matters related to armed conflict, conflict resolution, and peacekeeping. The members of the Review Group were: Dame Margaret Anstee, United Kingdom, former Special Representative of the Secretary-General in Angola; Christine Mary Chinkin, United Kingdom, Professor of Law, London School of Economics; Saran Daraba, Guinea, President, Mano River Women for Peace Network; Francis Deng, Sudan, Special Representative of the Secretary-General on internally displaced persons; Benita Diop, Senegal, President, Femmes Africa Solidarité; Savitri Goonesekere, Sri Lanka, Professor of Law, Member, Committee on the Elimination of Discrimination against Women; Dame Ann Hercus, New Zealand, former Special Representative of the Secretary-General in Cyprus; Devaki Jain, India, economist; Sujata Manohar, India, Member, National Human Rights Commission, former judge, Supreme Court of India; Binta Mansaray, Sierra Leone, Women's Commission for Refugee Women and Children; Muna Ndulo, Zambia, Professor of Law, Cornell Law School; Milena Pires, East Timor, member of the constituent assembly; Amanda Romero, Columbia, Quaker International Affairs Representative, Andean Region; Indai Lourdes Sajor, Philippines, human rights activist; Joan Seymour, Guyana, formerly with United Nations Department of Political Affairs; Danilo Türk, Slovenia, Assistant Secretary-General, United Nations Department of Political Affairs.

Two consultants, Dyan Mazurana, Research Scholar in Women's Studies, University of Montana, and Sandra Whitworth, Associate Professor of Political Science and Women's Studies, York University, made major contributions to the study.

I. Introduction

1.   On 31 October 2000, the Security Council adopted resolution 1325 (2000) on women, peace and security, which builds on the Presidential Statement of 8 March 2000 and a series of Council resolutions on children and armed conflict, the protection of civilians in armed conflict and the prevention of armed conflict.[1] On 24 and 25 October 2000, the Security Council held an open discussion on women, peace and security, in which 40 Member States made statements supporting the mainstreaming of gender perspectives into peace support operations and the participation of women in all aspects of peace processes.[2] The discussion followed an Arria Formula meeting[3] on women, peace and security on 23 October 2000 that afforded an opportunity for the members of the Council to discuss the impact of armed conflict on women, and the role of women in peace processes, with women representatives of non-governmental organizations (NGOs) from Guatemala, Sierra Leone, Somalia and Zambia. They presented the experiences of women and girls in armed conflict and also raised the concerns of grass-roots movements of women committed to preventing and solving conflicts, and bringing peace, security and sustainable development to their communities.

2.   In resolution 1325 (2000), the Security Council highlights the importance of bringing gender perspectives to the centre of all United Nations conflict prevention and resolution, peace-building, peacekeeping, rehabilitation and reconstruction efforts. The resolution invited the Secretary-General to carry out a study on the impact of armed conflict on women and girls, the role of women in peace-building and the gender dimensions of peace processes and conflict resolution. The present study has been prepared in response to that invitation. (See Annex for the full text of the resolution.)

Contemporary armed conflicts

3.   Armed conflicts continue to occur in many parts of the world and have escalated over the last decade.[4] In Africa, over one quarter of the continent's 53 countries were afflicted by conflict in the late 1990s.[5] Today's armed conflicts are predominantly internal, with regional and subregional repercussions; and the victims of those conflicts are dispro-

portionately civilians. While during the First World War, only 5 per cent of all casualties were civilians, during the 1990s civilians accounted for up to 90 per cent of casualties.[6] A recent study estimated that 3.2 million deaths occurred in internal armed conflicts from 1990 to 1995.[7]

4.   In contemporary conflicts civilians are targets. Mass displacement, use of child soldiers, and violence against ethnic and religious groups, as well as gender-based and sexual violence, are common. Increased access to inexpensive and lethal weaponry fuels and perpetuates armed conflict.[8] These weapons are used by State and non-State actors, irregular forces, private militias, guerillas, warlords and civilians.

5.   Civilians have been subjected to high levels of violence in contemporary conflicts, including through ethnic cleansing and genocide, torture, mutilation, abduction, amputation, execution, systematic rape as well as scorched earth tactics (such as the destruction of crops, villages and towns, and the poisoning of wells).[9] Civilians have sometimes been used as human shields by combatants and have been forced to flee, leaving behind their family members, their homes and possessions.

Women and contemporary armed conflict

6.   The specific experience of women and girls in armed conflict is linked to their status in societies. As noted in paragraph 135 of the Beijing Platform for Action, "while entire communities suffer the consequences of armed conflict and terrorism, women and girls are particularly affected because of their status in society and their sex". [10] Women do not enjoy equal status with men in any society. Where cultures of violence and discrimination against women and girls exist prior to conflict, they will be exacerbated during conflict. If women do not participate in the decision-making structures of a society, they are unlikely to become involved in decisions about the conflict or the peace process that follows.

7.   The changes in armed conflict over the last decade have affected women and girls. Women and girls are often viewed as bearers of cultural identity and thus become prime targets. Gender-based and sexual violence have increasingly become weapons of warfare and are one of the defining characteristics of contemporary armed conflict. Rape, forced impregnation, forced abortion, trafficking, sexual slavery and the intentional spread of sexually transmitted infections (STIs), including human immunodeficiency virus/acquired immunodeficiency syndrome (HIV/AIDS), are elements of contemporary conflict.

8.   Yet, women and girls are not only victims of armed conflict: they are also active agents and participants in conflict.[11] They may actively choose to participate in the conflict and carry out acts of violence because they are committed to the political, religious or economic goals of the parties to the conflict. Women and girls may also be manipulated into taking up military or violent roles (such as girl soldiers and female suicide bombers) through propaganda, abduction, intimidation and forced recruitment.

9.   Women and girls may also provide non-military support for war. They can directly support combatants through cooking and cleaning for soldiers, acting as porters and messengers and through performing other tasks required by militaries. They can also indirectly support war efforts by developing and disseminating propaganda, encouraging their children to go to war, voting for Governments that launch military campaigns and fomenting distrust.

10.   The agency of women and girls is also expressed through their activities in peace processes before, during and after conflicts. Many are involved in grass-roots efforts aimed at rebuilding the economic, political, social and cultural fabric of their societies. However, women and girls are normally excluded from all formalized peace processes, including negotiations, the formulation of peace accords and reconstruction plans. Even where women and girls were actively involved in sustaining and rebuilding local economies and communities throughout the conflict they are frequently pushed to the background when formal peace negotiations begin.[12] In the case where women have been involved in national peace negotiations they have often brought the perspectives of women and girls to the peace table,[13] for example, by ensuring that peace accords address demands for gender equality in new constitutional, judicial and electoral structures.

11.   While armed conflict and instability more often than not entail profound loss, stress and burden, women and girls can gain temporarily from the changed gender relations that may result from armed conflict. They can acquire new status, skills and power through taking on new responsibilities. These changes can challenge existing norms about their roles in society.[14] In some conflicts, the loss of men through exile, fighting or death has allowed women and girls to assume functions that were normally the prerogative of men. At such points, norms about roles and participation of women and girls in decision-making in the household, civil society, the formal economy, and

their rights to own land or goods may be altered, to their benefit.[15] Conflict may create space for a temporary redefinition of social relations, but often does not change them fundamentally. Gains made are usually reversed after the end of the conflict.

Incorporating gender perspectives in peace and security

12.   Gender refers to the socially constructed roles as ascribed to women and men, as opposed to biological and physical characteristics. Gender roles vary according to socio-economic, political and cultural contexts, and are affected by other factors, including age, race, class and ethnicity. Gender roles are learned and are changeable. Gender equality is a goal to ensure equal rights, responsibilities and opportunities of women and men, and girls and boys, which has been accepted by Governments and international organizations and is enshrined in international agreements and commitments.[16]

13.   Gender mainstreaming is the strategy established by Member States of the United Nations to achieve gender equality. Gender mainstreaming is defined in the Economic and Social Council agreed conclusions 1997/2 as: "the process of assessing the implications for women and men of any planned action, including legislation, policies or programmes in all areas and at all levels. It is a strategy for making the concerns and experiences of women and men an integral dimension of design, implementation, monitoring and evaluation of policies and programmes in all political, economic and societal spheres so that women and men benefit equally and inequality is not perpetuated. The ultimate goal is to achieve gender equality". Gender mainstreaming entails bringing the perceptions, experience, knowledge and interests of women and men to bear on policy-making, planning and decision-making. Mainstreaming does not replace the need for targeted, women-specific policies and programmes, and positive legislation; nor does it do away with the need for gender units or focal points.

14.   The Beijing Platform for Action notes, in paragraph 141, that "in addressing armed and other conflicts, an active and visible policy of mainstreaming a gender perspective into all policies and programmes should be promoted so that before decisions are taken an analysis is made of the effects on women and men, respectively". A focus on gender mainstreaming in conflict and post-conflict situations involves recognizing that women, girls, men and boys participate in and experience conflict, peace processes and post-conflict recovery differently.

These differences and inequalities should be understood and taken into account in all responses to conflict prevention, conflict situations and post-conflict rehabilitation and reconstruction.

15.   The increased participation of women within humanitarian, peace-building and peacekeeping operations is crucial if the United Nations goals and mandates regarding gender equality, non-discrimination and human rights are to be realized. Because of under-representation of women, particularly at decision-making levels, efforts are required to promote gender balance in United Nations work on peace and security. The United Nations is committed to a goal of 50:50 gender-balance in all posts at the professional level and above.[17]

United Nations initiatives on women, peace and security

16.   The United Nations has been increasingly responsive to the impact of armed conflict on women and girls. In 1969, the Commission on the Status of Women considered whether special protection should be accorded to women and children during armed conflict and emergency situations. In 1974, the General Assembly adopted the Declaration on the Protection of Women and Children in Emergency and Armed Conflict. The risks to women and children, and the importance of involving women in peace issues, were also recognized during the discussions at the United Nations Conference on Women in Mexico in 1975. During the International Decade for Women (1976 to1985) equality, development and peace were central themes, and the Nairobi Forward-Looking Strategies for the Advancement of Women, adopted at the 1985 Third World Conference on Women, advanced the discussion on women, peace and security. Throughout the 1980s, the United Nations increasingly took account of the impact of armed conflict on women, mothers and caregivers. However, this perspective did not reflect a full understanding of the differential impact of armed conflict on women and men.[18]

17.   The growing understanding of violence against women, generally and particularly in armed conflict, was contributed to by the findings of the Commission of Experts (the Yugoslav Commission) during the conflict in the former Yugoslavia, which collected information on violations of international humanitarian law, including over 1,100 reports of sexual violence.[19]

18.   In 1993, the Security Council established the International Criminal Tribunal for the former Yugoslavia (ICTY)[20] and in 1994 the International Criminal Tribunal for Rwanda (ICTR).[21] The Statutes and jurisprudence of the two ad hoc Tribunals, and the more recent Statutes of the International Criminal Court (ICC)[22] and the Special Court for Sierra Leone,[23] include provisions which reflect an understanding of the gender implications of armed conflict and are of landmark significance in the context of redress for women and girls through the international criminal law process.

19.   The 1993 United Nations World Conference on Human Rights, held at Vienna, recognized violence against women during armed conflict as a violation of human rights. The General Assembly adopted, in 1993, the Declaration on the Elimination of Violence against Women, which recognized that women in situations of armed conflict are especially vulnerable to violence.[24]

20.   The Fourth World Conference on Women, held in Beijing in 1995, identified women and armed conflict as one of the 12 critical areas of concern to be addressed by Member States, the international community and civil society. Paragraph 44 of the Beijing Platform for Action calls on "[g]overnments, the international community and civil society, including NGOs and the private sector... to take strategic action", inter alia, in relation to "[t]he effects of armed or other kinds of conflict on women, including those living under foreign occupation". This chapter of the Platform is reinforced by the critical areas of concern on violence against women and the human rights of women.

21.   The Platform for Action recognized, in paragraph 133, that civilian casualties outnumber military casualties, with women and children comprising a significant number of the victims, and proposed a number of strategic objectives and actions to be taken by relevant actors. Paragraph 145 of the Platform called for the upholding and reinforcement of the norms of international humanitarian and human rights law in relation to the offences against women, and the prosecution of all those responsible for such offences.

22.   The Commission on the Status of Women adopted agreed conclusions on women and armed conflict in 1998, which addressed gender-sensitive justice; the specific needs of women affected by armed conflict; the need to increase women's participation in all stages of

peace processes, including conflict prevention, post-conflict resolution and reconstruction; and disarmament issues.

23.   In 2000, the twenty-third special session of the General Assembly entitled "Women 2000: gender equality, development and peace for the twenty-first century",[25] reaffirmed the commitments made in the Beijing Declaration and Platform for Action. The outcome document called for the full participation of women at all levels of decision-making in peace processes, peacekeeping and peace-building. It also addressed the need to increase the protection of girls in armed conflict, especially the prohibition of their forced recruitment.

24.   In 1994, the United Nations Commission on Human Rights appointed a Special Rapporteur on violence against women, its causes and consequences. From the beginning of her work, the Special Rapporteur indicated that "all violations of the human rights of women in situations of armed conflict, and in particular, murder, systematic rape, sexual slavery and forced pregnancy ..." would be covered by her mandate.[26] The Special Rapporteur has presented a number of reports on violence against women in armed conflict to the Commission.[27] Notably, in March 2002, the Special Rapporteur briefed members of the Security Council on violence against women in Sierra Leone and highlighted the need to investigate, prosecute and punish those responsible for rape and other forms of gender-based violence.

25.   The Special Rapporteur on the question of systematic rape and sexual slavery and slavery-like practices during wartime, was appointed in 1995 by the Sub-Commission on the Promotion and Protection of Human Rights.[28] The Special Rapporteur submitted a final report in 1998 and an updated report in June 2000.[29] The 2000 report contains a detailed examination of what has been achieved in the progressive development of international criminal law to address gender-based crimes and sexual violence.

26.   The work of other Special Rapporteurs or Representatives has contributed to the growing understanding of the situation of women and girls during armed conflict. The Special Rapporteurs on the former Yugoslavia, Rwanda, the Democratic Republic of the Congo, as well as the Special Rapporteur on torture, have all highlighted gender-based and sexual violence against women and girls committed during armed conflicts.

27.   In 1992, the Secretary-General appointed the Special Representative on internally displaced persons to examine human rights issues relating to internal displacement. In 1998, the Special Representative formulated Guiding Principles on Internal Displacement, which have become the framework for policy and programmes for governmental and humanitarian actors in dealing with internal displacement. The Guiding Principles contain a number of provisions addressing the specific needs of women.

28.   In 1996, the Secretary-General's study[30] on the impact of armed conflict on children emphasized the roles and experiences of girls and highlighted the ways in which they are placed at high risk during armed conflict.

29.   In 1997, the Secretary-General appointed a Special Representative for Children in Armed Conflict with a mandate to protect and promote the rights of war-affected children and ensure that those rights are comprehensively addressed by the main actors at all levels. The efforts of the Special Representative for Children in Armed Conflict have resulted in the inclusion of child protection officers in the mandates of the United Nations peacekeeping missions in Sierra Leone and the Democratic Republic of the Congo. The Special Representative has also supported and facilitated the development of local peace initiatives, such as the Sudanese Women for Peace. He has included gender perspectives in his work, including through advocating for a new law in Rwanda allowing girls to inherit property.

30.   There have been a series of positive initiatives by the United Nations in addressing HIV/AIDS in conflict situations, including Security Council resolution 1308 (2000) on HIV/AIDS and international peace-keeping operations. In June 2001, the Security Council released a Presidential Statement welcoming references in the Declaration of Commitment[31] on HIV/AIDS with regard to situations of armed conflict and disasters, in particular the measures recommended to reduce the impact of conflict and disasters on the spread of HIV/AIDS.

31.   Intergovernmental bodies dealing with peace support operations have increasingly become aware of the importance of incorporating gender perspectives into their work, including the Security Council and the Special Committee on Peacekeeping Operations. This Special Committee first placed an item on gender mainstreaming on its agenda

at its session in 1999 and has since kept gender mainstreaming and gender balance issues under review.

32.   A thorough review of the United Nations peace and security activities was undertaken by a high-level Panel convened by the Secretary-General in 2000, which resulted in the Report of the Panel on the United Nations Peace Operations. The report recognized the need for equitable gender representation in the leadership of peacekeeping missions.[32] The seminar on the gender perspectives of multidimensional peacekeeping missions led to the development of the Windhoek Declaration and the Namibia Plan of Action on Mainstreaming a Gender Perspective in Multidimensional Peace Operations in June 2000.[33] The Windhoek Declaration was a critical step leading to the adoption of resolution 1325 (2000).

33.   The Security Council has increasingly focused its attention on issues related to the situation of children and armed conflict, the protection of civilians during armed conflict, as well as the prevention of armed con-flict. In March 2000, the Security Council issued a Presidential Statement on International Women's Day in March 2000. It recognized the link be-tween peace and gender equality and the fact that women's full participa-tion in peace operations was essential to sustainable peace. Following the adoption of resolution 1325 in 2000, the Council discussed women's role in peace processes again in October 2001, and adopted a Presidential Statement. Women, peace and security was discussed in an open debate in the Council on 25 July 2002. The Council adopted an aide-memoire[34] which identified 13 core objectives for protecting civilians in conflict situations, including the specific needs of women for assistance and pro-tection in 2002.

34.   The Council has sought to meet with women's groups and others in civil society in its missions to the Democratic Republic of the Congo, Kosovo and Sierra Leone to access information on the situation of women and girls. The Council requested the Special Rapporteur on violence against women to testify before the Council on the situation of women in Sierra Leone in March 2002. The Council has also used the Arria Formula meetings to inform its debates on women and peace processes. These meetings have included the views of women representatives of NGOs, from many war-torn areas, including Afghanistan, Guatemala, Kosovo, the Mano River area covering Guinea, Liberia and Sierra Leone, and from Israel and Palestine.

35.   Much progress has been made over the past 15 years to address the concerns of women and girls displaced from their homes and communities. The Inter-Agency Standing Committee (IASC) issued a policy statement for the integration of a gender perspective in humanitarian assistance in 1998 and developed a Plan of Action to address issues of sexual exploitation in humanitarian operations in 2002.

Objectives and focus of the study

36.   The study draws on existing research, and includes inputs from the United Nations, its specialized agencies, funds and programmes. Member States, scholars, and local and international NGOs. The preparation of the study was overseen by the Special Adviser of the Secretary-General on Gender Issues and Advancement of Women in cooperation with the Inter-Agency Task Force on Women, Peace and Security. In order to ensure that the study reflects a balanced range of experiences, and draws on as many regional perspectives as possible, a Review Group was established which provided additional inputs and reviewed drafts of the study.

37.   While many actors, including international and regional organizations, Member States and civil society, are involved in peace and security issues, the study focuses on the activities of the United Nations, and its specialized agencies, funds and programmes. It provides an overview of current responses to armed conflict by the United Nations system. Examples presented in the study are meant to be illustrative rather than comprehensive.

38.   The study emphasizes the roles of women and girls as victims and active agents during the conflict and in post-conflict reconstruction. Chapter II highlights how women and girls are affected by armed conflict differently than men and boys and points to the fact that women assume a variety of roles during conflict, including as civilians, combatants and peace activists. It describes the many forms of violence to which women and girls are exposed, including gender-based and sexual violence. It addresses the effect of armed conflict on the health of women and girls, the socio-economic dimensions of conflict and the situation of women as refugees, returnees and internally displaced persons.

39.   Chapter III provides an overview of the international law applicable in times of armed conflict – international humanitarian law and

human rights law, international criminal law and international refugee law. The chapter highlights legal developments, which have focused on the individual responsibility for abuses committed during armed conflict, particularly in the framework of the ad hoc international criminal tribunals and the ICC.

40.   Both informal and formal peace processes are discussed in Chapter IV, as well as the extent to which gender perspectives are being integrated into all aspects of peacemaking and peace-building of the United Nations. It highlights the ways in which women are often actively involved in informal peace processes, but are often largely absent from formal peace processes.

41.   Chapter V presents critical gender perspectives in peacekeeping operations, including in mandates, operations and recruitment. It analyzes the challenges to mainstreaming gender in all aspects of peacekeeping and highlights responses, including in training of staff, the contributions of gender advisers/units, and the importance of standards of conduct. A number of successful strategies of peacekeeping missions are presented which support capacity-building for women's political participation and address violence against women and trafficking.

42.   Chapter VI presents an overview of gender perspectives in humanitarian operations, including with regard to protection issues and prevention of violence, relief distribution and women's access to resources and benefits. It illustrates policies and strategies established and humanitarian activities undertaken by the United Nations system and civil society, to address the needs and priorities of women and girls. Current challenges are also highlighted.

43.   Chapter VII discusses the opportunities as well as the obstacles women and girls face in the reconstruction of political, civil, judicial, economic and social sectors and points to the importance of addressing gender perspectives in the transition from humanitarian to reconstruction efforts.

44.   Disarmament, demobilization and reintegration (DDR) initiatives are reviewed in Chapter VIII. Evidence from past DDR programmes indicate that women and girl combatants should be identified and their needs and priorities specifically addressed. The chapter sets out a range of issues that should be incorporated into these initiatives.

45.   The study includes a series of recommendations which are presented at the end of each chapter.

II. Impact of Armed Conflict on Women and Girls

46.   Understanding the impact of armed conflict on women and girls requires attention to four specific themes. First, women and girls tend to experience conflict differently than men and boys. There is growing awareness of the gender differences and inequalities during war and in post-conflict reconstruction. Yet it is misleading to set up a dichotomy that locates women and men in totally different spheres. Women and men share experiences and are intimately connected to each other through their families and communities. Women often see their needs and interests as interwoven with the needs and interests of their male partners and other family members.

47.   Second, women (just like men) are both actors and victims in armed conflicts. Women participate in armed forces as combatants and through playing supporting roles. They may assume these roles willingly or be forced to play them.[1] Between 1990 and 2002, girl soldiers were among fighting forces and groups in at least 54 countries, and fought in conflicts in 36 of those countries.[2] Women and adolescent girls may also support fighting forces and prolong the conflict in numerous other ways. They may infiltrate opposition groups for the purposes of passing information, hide or smuggle weapons, support or care for fighters. For example, in Sierra Leone, women supporting the rebel forces smuggled weapons through checkpoints in baskets of fish, under their clothing and via their children. They also infiltrated governmental and peacekeeping forces using social contacts.[3] Individual women combine various roles at once, such as displaced person, community activist, small business owner, soldier and homeless person.

48.   In many conflict situations, local civil society groups, including women's organizations and networks, actively work to halt the fighting, or address some of its worst effects. Their activities may be limited in countries where women do not have full and equal rights or are considered the property of their husbands and fathers.[4] Although these restrictions are usually tightened during armed conflict, women and adolescent girls continue to organize for change.[5] Women and girls are also peace activists, working to heal communities and bring about sustainable peace.

49.   Third, although this study often refers to "women and girls" and highlights many trends and observations that are common to conflicts across

countries, regions and continents, each situation must be understood on its own terms. Women are not a homogenous group and may have contradictory interests and priorities. The economic, social and political conditions also vary from country to country and it is crucial to ground programmatic responses in concrete realities.

50. Fourth, there is often confusion and misunderstanding of whether or not a gender analysis is the same as a focus on women. This study focuses on the experiences of women and girls. It has, however, used gender analysis as the basis for understanding what happens to women and girls in armed conflict and to develop effective operational responses.

A. Violence against women and girls

Threats to the personal safety of civilians

51. Civilian women and girls face different risks and dangers in armed conflict compared to those faced by civilian men and boys. There is a growing literature and attention to sexual violence and rape as a strategy of warfare. However, there are other forms of violence and security and protection issues that are important in conflict situations. As has been noted by the International Committee of the Red Cross (ICRC): "The fact, that generally, women do not go off to fight and largely remain unarmed and unprotected at a time when traditional forms of moral, community and institutional safeguard have disintegrated, and weapons have proliferated, leads to women being particularly vulnerable during wartime".[6]

52. Women and men often do different types of work, frequently as a result of prescribed gender roles, and may be exposed to different threats through this work. Women tend to be responsible for the care and nurture of the family and thus shoulder heavy burdens. Collection of firewood or water often puts young girls and women at risk of dangers, which include kidnapping, sexual abuse and exposure to landmines.

53. Social attitudes also affect the vulnerability of women and girls. For example, families have often wrongly assumed that an elderly woman or a woman with children will be safe from harm and have left them to safeguard property while the rest of the family flees.[7]

54. The torture of women and girls in armed conflict has been increasingly documented.[8] Women and adolescent girls have been tortured for holding prominent political or community positions, for speaking out

against opposing groups, or for resisting violence against themselves and their families. They have been targeted for being educators and for their roles as cultural symbols of their communities. They have been tortured as a means to attack the men in their lives, whether fathers, husbands, sons or intimates, rather than on account of their own actions or public identity. The torture of women and adolescent girls has been carried out to violate the victim's sense of herself as a person and as a woman.[9]

55.   Research conducted by the ICRC shows that small arms, if not removed following the cessation of conflict, may be directed towards the civilian population, or the weapons may be used in interpersonal violence. Armed conflict exacerbates existing inequalities between women and men and puts women and girls at heightened risk of physical and emotional abuse from male family members.[10] The increased availability of and access to weapons increases the risk of severe injury or death during assault.[11] Women-run SOS hotlines for abused women and children reported high levels of abuse during and following the wars in the former Yugoslavia, as weapons that men used during the war were turned on women and children when they returned home.[12]

56.   Given the gender-based division of labour, women and men have different risks of exposure to landmines. For example, women are at risk since they are responsible for gathering fuel or fetching water while men may be in greater danger on public roads.[13] Women who have lost their limbs may be unable to farm and are often abandoned by their husbands.[14] With men making up the majority of landmine casualties, women may be required to provide sole support for their families.[15]

57.   Even if women are not directly wounded during armed conflict, the devastation suffered by their families and the threat of violence can contribute to women's isolation. Widowhood, flight to cities and remaining inside the home to avoid violence, all serve to break down social institutions and isolate women.[16]

Gender-based and sexual violence

58.   During times of armed conflict, women and girls experience all physical, emotional and sexual forms of violence. Evidence from recent conflicts indicates that members of fighting forces have specifically targeted women, adolescent girls and, to a lesser extent, girl children.[17] The forms of violence used – torture, rape, mass rape, sexual slavery, enforced prostitution, forced sterilization and the forced termination of pregnancies, and mu-

tilations – and the ways in which perpetrators carry out these violent acts, are closely linked to gender relations in the society and culture.[18]

59.   Men and adolescent boys are also subject to gender-based and sexual torture. The sexual abuse, torture and mutilation of male detainees or prisoners is often carried out to attack and destroy their sense of masculinity or manhood. Abuse and torture of female members of a man's family in front of him is used to convey the message that he has failed in his role as protector.[19] These forms of humiliation and violence take on powerful political and symbolic meanings. The deliberate initiation and endorsement of these acts by military commanders and political leaders underscores the significance of these acts as more than random assaults.

60.   Throughout history women, adolescent girls and to a lesser extent girls have been subjected to rape, including mass rape. The raping of women is a means for the aggressor to symbolically and physically humiliate the defeated men.[20] Rape or the threat of rape is also used to drive communities off lands or to heighten terror during attacks. In recent years rape has also been used to wilfully transmit HIV.[21] In Sierra Leone, women and adolescent girls suffered beatings, food deprivation, and physical and sexual torture if they resisted rape by armed groups.[22] In Uganda, women and adolescent girls captured by the rebels "were routinely raped by numbers of rebels and any reluctance or attempt to resist usually meant summary execution".[23] Throughout the genocide in Rwanda, the rape and mutilation of women and girls by opposing groups was carried out, not only as an attack against these females, but as a means to exercise power over and demoralize the men in the women's family, clan and ethnic group.[24]

61.   Rape may be used to forcibly impregnate women and adolescent girls. In Bosnia and Herzegovina, rape, sexual violence and forced pregnancy were used as a form of ethnic cleansing. In some cases, forced pregnancy is a deliberate strategy of the armed forces to destroy ethnic groups, with women and adolescent girls being held against their will and repeatedly raped until they conceive, as in Bosnia and Herzegovina and Rwanda.[25]

62.   Sexual slavery is another form of gender-based violence experienced by women and girls during armed conflict. Examples of women and adolescent girls being forced into sexual slavery include East Timorese women abducted during the occupation of the island region, and Rwandan "ceiling women" who were kept in the space between the rafters and roof while their captors were away and then brought down for sexual and domestic slave labour upon the captors' return.[26] Women and adolescent girls are also forced to serve as

sexual slaves when they are abducted and given as "wives" to reward fighters. The sexual abuse of women and adolescent girls who have been abducted by fighting forces and groups appears widespread, as in the Democratic Republic of the Congo, Sierra Leone and Uganda.[27]

63.   The international presence which follows armed conflict has been linked to an increasing demand for prostitution and trafficking of women and girls.[28] For example, an investigation of refugee camps in Guinea, Liberia and Sierra Leone revealed the sexual exploitation of women, girls and boys by humanitarian workers and peacekeepers in exchange for basic provisions.[29]

Trafficking in women and girls

64.   The International Organization for Migration (IOM) estimates that, in 2001, between 700,000 and 2 million women and children were trafficked across international borders.[30] There is increasing evidence that a significant amount of this activity is associated with armed conflict. Trafficking in human beings involves the recruitment, transportation, transfer and harbouring of persons for the purpose of exploitation, including prostitution, sexual exploitation, forced labour and slavery. Trafficked women and girls face severely compromised physical and mental health, in particular reproductive health problems due to rape, sexual abuse, STIs, including HIV/AIDS, trauma and unwanted pregnancies.[31]

65.   The conditions that push women and girls into forced labour, trafficking and other forms of exploitation stem from a combination of internal and external factors. Pre-war systems of gender inequality, war economies, criminal syndicates, and the destruction and destabilization of livelihoods combine to place women and girls at high risk of trafficking. Trafficking is fostered by transition, instability, poverty, disintegrating social networks, and disintegrating law and order in sending, transit and receiving countries. Corruption contributes to trafficking. The inefficiency, as well as the complicity of the law enforcement and military personnel in some countries, allow traffickers to function since they do not fear arrest, prosecution or conviction.

66.   Women and girls are also trafficked within and across borders to sexually service combatants.[32] In some cases of international trafficking, women and girls are sold into camps of rebels or soldiers. In countries directly affected by war, women and girls may be lured by offers of protection and access to safety zones, or deliberately abducted to work for militias in economic activities, such as diamond and gem mining which support the conflict. In Sierra Leone, women were used as sexual slaves for the camp

managers and forced to grow food, cook and provide other services. In the Democratic Republic of the Congo and Liberia, women and children were abducted to work for the many militias that patrol the diamond fields, as well as to service the commanders. The conditions in Afghanistan resulted in women and young girls being trafficked into India, Pakistan and, to a lesser degree, other countries in Central Asia.[33] International intervention itself can result in an increase in trafficking operations and may intensify during post-conflict periods.

B. Health of women and girls

67.   Women and girls are wounded and killed in armed conflict just like men and boys. Women and girls also face health threats that stem from biological differences. For example, the physical vulnerability of women and adolescent girls is higher than that of men and adolescent boys due to their sexual and reproductive roles. Particular risks women face include STIs, including HIV/AIDS and "vesico-vaginal fistula, trauma, mutilation, complications from botched abortions, uterine problems, scarring of the vagina and problems having a normal sexual life or giving birth in the future",[34] which are exacerbated in conflict situations.

68.   Pregnant and lactating mothers require additional nutritional and physical care. In many conflict situations, the additional energy and micronutrient needs of pregnant mothers are not met. The resulting high rates of low birth weight increase the risk for children of death during the first months of life, impaired immune function, poor cognitive development, and chronic diseases later on in adulthood. Complications during pregnancy, childbirth, and breastfeeding are often untreated due to the destruction or lack of medical and health facilities and personnel. Such complications can result in high maternal and infant mortality rates, as evidenced in Afghanistan and Sierra Leone. Dangerous birthing practices and lack of access to trained midwives may result in higher death rates for women and adolescent girls, especially among abducted adolescent girls and first-time mothers, as reported in Sierra Leone.[35]

69.   There are other health issues that relate specifically to gender roles and identities. For example, during famine or food shortages, women and girls are more susceptible to malnutrition than men because of inequitable distribution of food within households and at the community level. The combination of malnutrition and gender-based discrimination may result in the stunted growth and development in adolescent girls and girl children

and contribute to additional health risks for pregnant or lactating mothers, and in some cases result in death. In a Bangladeshi refugee camp, Rohingya girls under one year of age were dying at twice the rate of boys, and among refugee children under five, girls were dying at 3.5 times the rate of boys.[36] Crowding, poor housing conditions and inadequate sanitation within villages, towns, or camps often increases rates of and exposure to malaria, tuberculosis, and other communicable diseases.

70.   In situations of armed conflict, severe mental and social stress can be caused by death, separation and loss of family and friends; loss of home and social environment; exposure to violence, including witnessing or directly experiencing rape, torture, and the killing of friends or relatives; the weakening or severing of family and community bonds and networks; destruction of basic infrastructure; loss of economic livelihood opportunities; and material deprivation. In the context of conflicts which are prolonged for many years, populations experience longer exposure to extreme stressors. Children live deprived of caring adults; parents experience anxiety about their ability to protect and provide for their children; and adolescent heads of households fear for their safety and that of their siblings.

71.   The psychological and social impacts of armed conflict are intertwined. Changes in social interactions may create psychological distress. Studies have shown the grave consequences of gender-based social repression on the psychological well-being of women. In a study on women's health in Afghanistan during the Taliban regime, interviewees attributed their depression to Taliban policies that restricted their movement, access to employment and education opportunities, and caused isolation, financial hardship and fear. Among the study group, 65 per cent of the women reported considering suicide, and 16 per cent reported having attempted to commit suicide.[37]

72.   Although in many respects nuclear, biological and chemical weapons affect women and men in a similar manner, there are some important differences, mostly relating to health. This is particularly so in relation to weapons which may continue to have an impact on people long after the armed conflict has ended. There is some evidence of a differential impact on the physical and reproductive health of women of the use of chemical weapons. Women exposed to dioxin experienced higher rates of birth defects.[38]

73.   The looting and destruction of health care facilities, schools, public offices and other infrastructure during armed conflict makes it difficult for most people living in those areas to meet their basic needs. Many women

and girls are unable to obtain adequate medical care, because medical facilities are destroyed or poorly equipped and staffed, or because they cannot afford treatment. Medical care is not limited to physical service delivery, but also involves the provision of information. Women and girls are often left without vital information on the prevention of STIs, including HIV/AIDS, and pregnancy.[39]

HIV/AIDS

74. HIV/AIDS has been recognized by the Security Council and the Secretary-General as a serious threat to peace and security. In addition to the direct impact on people with HIV/AIDS, the death of parents, teachers, health and social workers, public and government officials, traditional leaders and healers due to HIV/AIDS and armed conflict undercut the institutions that could otherwise be working to mitigate and address the effects of these devastating forces. In sub-Saharan Africa, women are more likely than men to be infected with HIV. Infection rates among young women are four times as high as those of young men in some countries. Women continue to bear the burden of care for family members with HIV/AIDS. Women, including many elderly women, often assume the responsibility for children orphaned by AIDS.

75. Women and adolescents have the highest rates of new HIV infection. Mother-to-child transmission of HIV, either during birth or breastfeeding, contributes to increased infant and child mortality. At the same time, women and girls may have limited access to HIV/AIDS education and prevention, because of taboos around discussions of gender-based inequalities and sexuality, which limit their ability to make sexual and reproductive decisions free of discrimination, coercion and violence. [40]

76. The use of sexual violence as a strategic and tactical weapon of war contributes to the spread of STIs, including HIV/AIDS. In Sierra Leone, it is estimated that 70 per cent to 90 per cent of rape survivors had contracted STIs. Abducted girls were at a particularly high risk due to the many episodes of sexual violence. Fear of stigma related to sexual or reproductive health may prevent women and girls from seeking testing for HIV or health care. When available, the financial cost of treatment and care may be out of reach of most.[41]

77. Systematic gender-based discrimination inhibits the ability of women and girls to protect themselves from HIV infection or to respond fully to the consequences of infection for themselves and their families. The lack of control of women and adolescent girls over their sexuality, their inequality

within families and their inability to utilize legal mechanisms to uphold their rights also exacerbates this situation.[42]

78.   Looking at HIV/AIDS in conflict settings through a human rights lens highlights the importance of prevention. In the absence of functioning health and education systems in conflict situations, ensuring that women and girls have access to public information about HIV/AIDS and related services is crucial to stemming the spread and alleviating the devastating impact of HIV/AIDS. Awareness campaigns for women in camps for refugees and internally displaced persons (IDPs) can also encourage women to educate others about HIV/AIDS in their communities after they return home.

The response to gender-based and sexual violence

79.   The sexual violence experienced by women and adolescent girls has serious health consequences. Many societies blame the victim of sexual violence, particularly when the victim is a woman or girl. The resulting social rejection reinforces feelings of shame, guilt, loneliness and depression. Victims of gender-based violence may feel overcome with terror, experience a sense of powerlessness, worthlessness, apathy and denial.[43] In some societies, the stigma attached to sexual violation leads to ostracism and isolation. Husbands or family members may shun women or girls who acknowledge that they were raped.[44] Ostracism may also occur in societies that maintain certain myths about survivors of gender-based violence, such as in Sierra Leone, where it is believed that raped women and adolescent girls will become barren, sexually obsessed, and unable to remain faithful to their husbands.

80.   Healing is often fostered by allaying fears and building hope for the future. Integrated interventions which focus on the psychological, as well as the social, political and economic situations, are usually more successful. Experience has shown that recovery is dependent on a safe and supportive environment, a return to normal routines of life and the re-establishment of former supportive relationships or the establishment of new relationships. Experience has also shown the importance of ensuring that the intervention is appropriate in the specific context rather than rapidly imported from another context. Addressing everyday difficulties, such as reuniting families that have been separated, or assisting people to regain their economic livelihoods, can successfully mitigate the impact of trauma. During the war in the former Yugoslavia, for instance, many Western agencies arrived in Croatia and Bosnia and Herzegovina with plans to counsel women victims of rape. Those who took care to listen to the women, however, learnt that what was first and foremost on their minds was the desire to receive news of the

whereabouts of their husbands and other missing family members, or to get information on access to adequate supplies of milk or medical care for their babies. Some NGOs supplied radios so that the women could receive news from the frontlines. Access to basic nutrition and services for their children raised women's sense of security as a provider.

81.   If there is no guarantee of follow-up support, interventions that single out women and girls victims of sexual violence may further traumatize them. In situations where acknowledging rape has serious social consequences for the victim, it could be dangerous for the survivor to disclose information. During the conflict in the former Yugoslavia, there were documented cases of women attempting suicide after being pushed to disclose that they had been raped.[45] War-affected women and adolescent girls need a supportive community, where they find it safe to talk and are guaranteed confidentiality. Ensuring that men are involved and supportive is an important element.

82.   Education can increase a young girl's psychosocial well-being. In a research study carried out in Ingushetia, Russian Federation, parents, community members and the children themselves have indicated that access to education and the psychosocial activities not only educated them but also healed their minds and allowed them to concentrate on something besides the loss and continuing uncertainty and violence.[46]

C. Socio-economic dimensions

83.   Illicit trading of natural resources by parties to conflict has led to the emergence of specific forms of economic organization and divisions of labour. This allows the continuation of the conflict and diverts resources that could be used in a more beneficial manner. Women and girls who remain in conflict zones may find themselves with few options apart from working for warlords and criminal militias or entering into exploitative informal economies. Indentured servitude and other forms of forced labour may evolve along gender and generational lines. Apart from being used as sexual slaves for militia commanders and soldiers in Angola and the Democratic Republic of the Congo, women and adolescent girls are forced to do domestic work for soldiers, to work as daily labourers and to carry supplies and messages between work gangs or among fighting forces. Often these activities are used to further humiliate women under the control of armed forces.[47]

84.   As part of the assault on civilian livelihoods, wells are poisoned, lands are mined and market places destroyed, making the daily tasks of fetching water, tilling the land and buying and selling in markets increasingly dan-

gerous.[48] Functioning nurseries and schools are rare and qualified teachers are few, especially for the internally displaced and refugees.[49] With the deliberate bombing of schools and hospitals, responsibility for education and health is shifted back into the private sphere and to women. Women, as providers and caregivers, find that their workloads increase as the availability of resources and access to public and household goods shrink.

85.   Female enrolment in schools often drops in times of war because girl children and adolescents alike are forced to assume greater responsibilities to ensure household food security, for example, by working agricultural lands, carrying out domestic labour or undertaking work in the informal sector. As household resources decrease, adolescent girls are married off at younger and younger ages. Seeing few options for survival, adolescent girls may "choose" to marry older men.[50] Civil war compounded by environmental factors, most notably drought, in Somalia, the Sudan and Uganda, for example, has resulted in higher levels of child marriages.[51] Girls may also be sent off to work as domestics for little or no compensation, where they are at risk of sexual abuse from their masters.

86.   Armed conflict also changes social structures, networks and relations, particularly for women and girls. Displacement due to armed conflict increases the number of female and child-headed households, with the greatest increase in households headed by widows and children because adolescent and adult males have fled, gone into exile, joined fighting forces or have died or disappeared.[52] This may lead to an increase of work for the women who are forced to barter for the labour of other men to help prepare their fields.[53]

87.   The number of child-headed households grows during armed conflict. Children heading households face enormous challenges in trying to acquire material goods to sustain their families, such as food, clothing, household equipment or agricultural tools.[54] During times of armed conflict, they must compete with adults over increasingly scarce resources. Girl heads of households are particularly marginalized in such situations.[55] Such girls experience low status as female adolescents, the social stigma of being without parents, and the lack of protection – all factors intensified during armed conflicts.[56] Girl heads of households may also face additional risk when leaving the relative safety of their village or town to search for food or fuel. In trying to gather materials for the survival of their families, they may have to fend off sexual advances, harassment and abuse. Additionally, girls who head households are at an extremely high risk of contracting HIV as a result

of rape and coerced sex.[57] Many children within child-headed families do not attend school.[58]

88. Women are often the first to become unemployed or under-employed in conflict situations. Women may provide the primary or only source of income for their families. In response to the stresses produced by the collapse in livelihood systems, women and adolescent girls may pursue new and non-traditional occupations, including work normally done by men and military service. Women and adolescent girls have to work as daily labourers on State-owned or private plantations, replacing men and adolescent boys who are either in exile, in the militias or have been killed during conflict. In some war-affected societies, cross-border trade has increased as a result of the participation by women, many replacing former networks that had traditionally been run by men. In Chad, for example, women utilized the networks formed during their stay in refugee camps to do extensive cross-border trading in Nigeria and the Sudan. In pastoral communities in Eritrea, north-east Kenya and the Sudan, women have expanded their traditional trade in milk products to include items, such as handicrafts, beer, incense and other products traditionally sold by men.

89. With few options available, women and girls enter the informal sector and take poorly paying jobs, including selling home-prepared food and drink, making or washing clothes, caring for children and going into domestic service for wealthier families. While the informal sector offers important opportunities for income-generating activities essential for survival, it is not without risk. Women and girls who rely on casual labour and petty trade, enjoy no labour protections and are exposed to exploitation and danger.

90. Women and girls may turn to illegal activities, including prostitution, brewing of alcohol and trafficking of drugs, which provide lucrative opportunities, but carry a high risk of violence.[59] These activities are often controlled by organized criminal elements that are closely integrated with militias and warlords relying on destabilized environments that support such illegal pursuits. In Somalia, some women resorted to banditry and looting.[60] In some countries, the conflict has caused an increase in child prostitution, beginning at the age of five. Women have to resort to smuggling and begging.

91. Looting, forcible displacement, roving fighting forces, and the threat of sniper fire, landmines and unexploded ordnance disrupt rural subsistence strategies. The breakdown of marketing structures, the destruction of marketplaces, and the looting and burning of seeds, crops and livestock, limit possibilities for agricultural production and trading. In order to survive,

communities resort to flight, foraging and sub-optimal coping strategies. Because of food insecurity, women and girls skip meals, adopt a less diverse diet, and reduce portions in order to protect the nutritional status of other family members, such as able-bodied men or young children, depending upon cultural norms. Women and adolescent girls cook less frequently because of fuel shortages or limited food supply, and integrate inferior food stuffs into their and their family's diets. In some conflict areas, so-called "famine foods", foods that are eaten only in times of severe food insecurity, are introduced into the diet. These foods have poor nutritional content and often require extensive preparation to decrease toxicity; for example, they require much time for soaking or cooking. These added requirements for food preparation further increase the workload as well as the risk of violence for girls, who are normally tasked with collecting fuel and water for household needs.

92.   Household assets are frequently sold in order to support families during conflict. In rural areas, this can include the sale of crops, seeds, water rights, land, farm animals and equipment. The loss of the personal assets of women and girls threatens the livelihood of the entire family. For example, the sale of women's jewelry, often a measure of family security, is a sign of extreme stress within a household, and leaves women and their families feeling vulnerable and exposed to greater risks.[61] Giving very young daughters away in marriage for a bride price, or knowingly selling them off to human traffickers, are other coping strategies in economically desperate households.

D. Displacement: women and girls as refugees, returnees and internally displaced persons

93. In 2001, the United Nations High Commissioner for Refugees (UNHCR) reported that there were 19.8 million refugees, asylum-seekers and others of concern to the Organization.[62] UNHCR also estimates that women and children constitute 80 per cent of the world's refugees and IDPs.

94.   Each phase of displacement, including initial displacement, flight, protection and assistance in refugee and displaced persons camps, resettlement and reintegration has different implications for female and male refugees and IDPs. Flight is often triggered by severe sex discrimination and gender-based persecution which may combine with discrimination and abuse on other grounds, such as ethnicity, religion and class. Refugee, returnee and internally displaced women and girls often suffer discrimination

and human rights abuses throughout their flight, settlement and return. For example, women and girls may be forced into providing sexual services to men and adolescent boys in exchange for safe passage for themselves or their family or to obtain necessary documentation or other assistance.[63] Children are at an increased risk of becoming separated from their parents, families or guardians. Girl children who become separated from their parents may face the risk of sexual abuse and being forced to serve in fighting forces and groups.

95.   In both refugee and IDP camps, women and girls can be at risk of human rights abuses due to the weakening of existing community and family protection mechanisms. Internally displaced women and girls are subjected to "physical and sexual attacks, rape, domestic violence and sexual harassment, increased spousal battering and marital rape".[64] For example, in Liberia, among the more than 1 million returning internally displaced persons were many women and girls who were struggling with the consequences of rape and unwanted pregnancies.

96.   Increased militarization and the presence of both civilians and combatants in camps heighten insecurity for all refugees and IDPs. Poorly lit camps, or those that lack adequate security, place women and girls at heightened risk of attack by males inside and outside of the camps. Responsibilities of women and girls heighten their risk of injury outside the camp.

97.   Crossing mine fields or walking near military encampments to search for water and firewood, for example, subjects them to risk of injury from landmines, crossfire and sexual attacks. According to reports from camps in northern Uganda, women and girls have to spend hours collecting water, which puts them at risk of abduction and sexual assault.[65]

98.   Both refugee and internally displaced women and girls may become victims of hostage-taking for purposes of enslavement and trafficking into slavery, coerced or enforced prostitution, abduction and forced military recruitment for participation in hostilities or support of combatants. Refugee and internally displaced women and adolescent girls may also be subjected to forced marriages and to being sold into marriage. They may be victimized through slavery and rape and may be forcibly recruited into armies.[66]

99.   One of the most negative impacts of uprooting is the weakening or loss of social support networks. This has several consequences for uprooted women and girls which have security implications relating to the ability to live free from harassment or abuse, to escape, to defend oneself or to gain access to the assistance and protection necessary to survive.[67] These conse-

quences may result in sexual exploitation. Furthermore, the establishment of orphanages for war-affected children separated from their families and communities may create conditions conducive to trafficking in children, particularly girls.

100. During the determination of refugee status and other asylum procedures that those seeking refuge encounter upon arrival, lack of knowledge about the effect of trauma and the cultural barriers to openly discussing traumatic experiences, particularly of sexual violence, can result in discriminatory treatment. Furthermore, domestic laws and policies on immigration that do not address the differential impact of armed conflict on women and girls may force them to return to their countries, despite the fact that they risk further violence and discrimination. Women and girls may also be forced to continue in abusive marriages in order to avoid withdrawal of visas and forced return to countries in conflict. In circumstances referred to as "refuge", "asylum" or "safe haven", the combination of generalized insecurity in uprooted communities and gender-blind programming can combine to create threatening experiences for women, adolescents and children who are at the greatest risk. Other central issues are the issuance of identity cards – whether women and children are granted their own or whether the male "head-of-household" retains all cards.

101. In conflict situations adults need protection and are less able to support and defend their families. Women and adolescent girls usually have to take up additional responsibilities if families and communities are split up. Men and adolescent boys in camps and settlements for refugees and internally displaced persons, on the other hand, often suffer from a dangerous level of inactivity. This volatile combination of overburden for some and inactivity and consequent frustration for others can become explosive. Incidents of domestic violence can escalate. For example, all married women interviewed in Burundi reported that they had experienced domestic violence during their time as refugees.[68]

102. Corruption or inequitable access to essential goods and services has had a negative effect on the nutritional status, personal security and physical and mental health of women and girls in refugee and internally displaced situations. When humanitarian assistance is not based on consultation with women and does not take their needs into account, women and girls may be left with few options and forced to turn to prostitution in exchange for goods and services.

103. Difficulties faced by refugee and internally displaced women and girls are often neglected within camp communities. This is especially true for those concerning sexual harassment or violence, domestic violence, and issues relating to sexual and reproductive health. At times there is inadequate or non-existent provision to maintain hygiene during menstruation. This has resulted in adolescent girls not attending school and women missing the distribution of assistance. Other issues include separate latrines for males and females, ensuring that latrine doors close properly and appropriate places to dispose of feminine hygiene materials.[69]

104. In situations of rape, some women and adolescent girls may be pressured or forced to abort, as occurred in IDP camps in Cambodia. Pregnant women and girls may seek illegal and unsafe abortions. Those who give birth may do so under unsafe and unhygienic conditions, with first-time mothers at heightened risk. Little is known about the children who are born of forced pregnancy or how women and adolescent girls with these children reintegrate in their communities.[70]

105. Distribution of food directly to women in camps helps to ensure that food is consumed by the target groups and is not diverted for other purposes, thus enhancing food security in families. Food security can also require the provision and maintenance of water points and grinding mills and the consideration of protection concerns associated with the collection of water and firewood. Neglect of these issues presents risks to women within the uprooted community and potential problems with the host community.

106. Ensuring security of livelihoods, access to economic activities and training in survival skills, health issues, leadership, and conflict resolution is important for the ability of refugee and internally displaced women and girls to cope under difficult circumstances and to ensure their sense of dignity and self-esteem. Without secure livelihood opportunities, recourse to prostitution becomes more common. In Colombia, for instance, large numbers of internally displaced women and adolescent girls reported that they had no alternative but prostitution to support themselves.[71]

107. Increasing the involvement of women and adolescent girls in the planning and management of camp life is necessary to meet the priorities and needs of women and girls as well as to ensure effective camp management. The participation of women in decisions regarding the organization of camps, the layout of shelters and facilities, and the distribution of supplies is critical to reducing the risks women and girls face in camp situations. Such risks include sexual exploitation by camp managers or displaced men

in charge of distributing the essentials for survival; the provision of inappropriate clothing to women and girls which puts them at risk of marginalization and physical abuse by all or part of the community; the rape and murder of women and children who go unprotected outside the camp perimeter in search of water, food or firewood; and the rape of unaccompanied women and girls concentrated in one area of a camp without supplemental protection.[72]

108. Refugees and internally displaced can be subject to cultural biases, especially in contexts where there is a marked difference in the cultures of the refugees and the host community. In camps where protection of refugees is weak, "culture" has been sometimes used to explain away certain crimes, resulting in a failure to address the issues of security and protection. There have been instances where prostitution, brewing of alcohol, trafficking in drugs and other illegal activities have been considered "normal" activities – part of the refugees' culture and background – by authorities responsible for the camps, despite the fact that they lead to an increase in gender-based violence.

E. Disappearance and detention

109. While the last 15 years have revealed the specific vulnerabilities to sexual violence in armed conflict, there has been less emphasis of the effect of armed conflict, such as detention and disappearances. Women and girls have "disappeared" in numerous conflicts in the last decade, including in Bosnia and Herzegovina, Croatia, Kosovo and Rwanda. The "disappearance" of male relatives affects women's status in their societies and traumatizes women who cannot find closure as long as they are hoping for the return of their relatives.

110. In many cultures the value of women or girls depends on their civil or family status. Information about relatives is thus not only critical to their emotional well-being; it can have a direct bearing on their personal security. For example, a woman living without a man may be unable to support the family, or may find herself the target of sexual attacks because of her unaccompanied status. Women or adolescent girls whose husbands are "disappeared" may experience many of the same hardships as widows while lacking the legal status of widow.[73] Successful tracing of missing or separated relatives is one of the most effective ways of improving the protection of and assistance to all uprooted persons. Survivors of the "disappeared" have the legal and ethical right to know the fate of their relatives.[74]

111. ICRC defines a detainee as "anyone held in custody by a detaining authority and regardless of whether or not the person has been tried and/or sentenced".[75] According to the ICRC, women are estimated to constitute four to five per cent of the population of the detained.[76] Adults and children are detained for a variety of reasons in armed conflict, including being directly involved in the conflict or for security reasons. Women may be detained as prisoners of wars, as civilian internees, as security detainees or for reasons related to social conduct.

112. Female detainees may experience a number of specific problems, including separation from their children, and prohibition of family visits. The lack of provisions in international instruments regarding whether, or at what age, children can stay with their mother or father in detention puts those children at risk of enforced separation or disappearance. Separations are, at times, undertaken to put pressure on the parent or to give the child to other couples who are supportive of the authorities.[77]

113. Because detaining authorities do not always provide enough material goods to sustain detainees in good health, the detained rely heavily on the support of family members, and international and NGOs. When male family members are detained, women and adolescent girls are often responsible not only for the additional burdens at home and in the marketplace, but also must prepare and take food and other items to their family members. Women and girls whose family members or partners have been imprisoned as a result of the conflict are often marginalized and are looked upon with mistrust, suspicion and resentment.[78] They may also face abuse from detaining authorities when they visit their family members.

F. Challenges to gender roles and relations

114. One of the ongoing discussions around women and armed conflict relates to the potential of building more equitable gender relations in post-conflict societies. It is argued that war breaks down traditions and communities but also opens new spaces for women. It is pointed out that women take on new tasks – often non-traditional tasks – and thus gain a new degree of freedom, flexibility and opportunity. Positive changes in social relationships, including gender relations have been reported, for example, in Chad.[79]

115. Others argue that building equitable gender relations and societies based on equality between women and men – a task that is fraught with difficulty even in times of peace – is difficult to achieve in the deprivation and chaos that follows conflict. More work is needed but recent research high-

lights the challenges that are faced when trying to further women's advancement after a conflict. Case studies carried out in Angola, Eritrea, Mali, Rwanda, Somalia and Sudan concluded that gender power structures changed as a result of conflict, but only to a limited degree. "Women's increased economic power has sometimes increased their scope for influence and action, mainly within but sometimes also outside the household. Changes in consciousness among women have resulted in the formation of women's associations. However, in general, changes in gender roles at micro level have not been accompanied by corresponding changes in political or organizational influence".[80]

Recommendations

Action 1:   Recognize the extent of violations of the human rights of women and girls during armed conflict; take measures to prevent such violations; provide appropriate redress and prosecute perpetrators; provide support to victims; and ensure that awareness of these violations informs planning and implementation in all peace support operations, humanitarian activities and reconstruction efforts.

Action 2:   Increase awareness of the risk for domestic violence and other threats to the personal safety of women and girls in post-conflict contexts and develop capacity to prevent and address such threats, including by training of all United Nations personnel and local police and military.

Action 3:   Identify and utilize local sources of information on the impact of armed conflict, and the impact of interventions – peacekeeping, peace-building, humanitarian operations, disarmament, demobilization and reintegration programmes, and reconstruction – on women and girls, and on the roles and contributions of women and girls in conflict situations, including through the establishment of regular contacts with women's groups and networks.

Action 4:   Ensure that all initial appraisals, assessments and fact-finding missions give attention to the situation of women and girls in conflict and post-conflict contexts so that analyses, data collection, planning processes which form the basis for the establishment of missions and programmes give adequate attention to their needs and priorities.

Action 5:   Incorporate information on the impact of armed conflict, and the impact of interventions – peacekeeping, peace-building, humanitarian, DDR, and reconstruction – on women and girls, and on the roles and contributions of women and girls in conflict situations, into all training provided to staff.

Action 6:   Promote, through existing executive bodies and inter-agency coordination mechanisms, such as the Executive Committee on Peace and Security, the Executive Committee on Humanitarian Affairs, the Executive Committee on Economic and Social Affairs, the United Nations Development Group, the Inter-Agency Standing Committee and the Inter-Agency Network on Women and Gender Equality, the strengthening of collaboration and coordination on addressing the impact of armed conflict on women and girls, including through the exchange of information and good practice examples – for example on policies, strategies, guidelines and codes of conduct, and through increased monitoring and reporting on the implementation of gender mainstreaming in all peace support activities.

Action 7:   Undertake an annual review of the implementation of resolution 1325 (2000) and report to the Security Council.

III. International Legal Framework

116. International law provides a framework of protection for individuals affected by armed conflict. International humanitarian law, the body of law which comes into operation at the outbreak of international or non-international armed conflict, regulates the conduct of hostilities and protects those who are not taking part in hostilities or are no longer doing so. It is the area of law that is of primary relevance to the protection of women and girls during armed conflict. International human rights law is also applicable in times of armed conflict, and is of particular importance in the context of internal armed conflict, where international humanitarian law may not apply. International criminal law has also come to assume increasing significance in relation to crimes against women and girls during armed conflict, in particular crimes of sexual violence. The protections offered by the provisions of international refugee law are also of relevance to women and girls prior to, during and in the aftermath, of armed conflict.

117. The following chapter provides an overview of the application of these complementary strands of international law. It also considers procedural innovations that address the particular needs of women and girl victims of international crimes in armed conflict. Avenues for compensation for war-related injuries, which is of particular relevance for women and girls as they seek to reconstruct their lives, are also described.

A. International humanitarian law and human rights law

118. International humanitarian law consists of both conventional and customary rules, the principal conventional instruments of relevance to the protection of victims of armed conflict being the four Geneva Conventions of 1949 and their two Additional Protocols of 1977, which deal with international armed conflicts and non-international armed conflicts respectively.[1] International humanitarian law is binding on both States and organized groups. Many of the rules provided by these treaties form part of customary international law, and are thus binding on all States.

119. The protections and guarantees laid down by the Geneva Conventions and their Additional Protocols are granted to all without discrimination. Accordingly, women combatants and civilians enjoy the protection of the general rules of international humanitarian law on a basis of equality with men.

Some of the provisions of international humanitarian law are of particular importance to women, including those relating to the maintenance and restoration of family ties (Geneva IV, Article 26; Protocol I, Article 32). The Conventions and their Additional Protocols also include special provisions that offer additional protection to women. These require women to be treated with all consideration due to their sex (Geneva I, Article 12; Geneva II, Article 12; Geneva III, Article 14, Protocol I, Article 76), and seek to reduce their vulnerability to sexual violence, or provide protections for pregnant women and mothers of young children. There are no special provisions in relation to women in the rules determining the legitimate conduct of hostilities.

120.   The conventional rules proscribe any attacks on the "honour" of civilian women, with Article 27 of the Fourth Geneva Convention pro-viding that such women are to be "especially protected ... in particular against rape, enforced prostitution or any form of indecent assault". Article 27 does not protect women from the activities of the State of which they are a national, but Protocol I extends protection to all who are in the territory of a party to a conflict. Article 75.2 of that Protocol prohibits, in relation to both women and men "outrages upon personal dignity, in particular humiliating and degrading treatment, enforced prostitution and any form of indecent assault", whether committed by military or civilian personnel. Article 76 of the Protocol applies specifically to women, and provides that women "shall be the object of special respect and shall be protected in particular against rape, forced prostitution and any other forms of indecent assault". Female prisoners-of-war, internees and detainees are to be treated with all the regard due to their sex, and are to be provided with female supervision and accommodation and sanitary conveniences separate from those provided to men (Geneva III, Articles 13; 25; 29; 85; 97; and 108; see also Protocol I, 75.6; Protocol 5 (2)). Punishments in excess of those applicable to male prisoners-of-war may not be imposed on women prisoners (Geneva III, Article 88).

121.   Additional protection is provided to pregnant women and mothers of young children (Geneva IV, Articles 18, 20 and 21). They are accorded special treatment in relation to medical care (Geneva IV, Articles 50 and 91; Protocol I, Article 70); food (Geneva IV, Articles 23, 50 and 89; Protocol I, Article 70); physical safety (Geneva IV, Articles 14, 17, 18, 20 and 21); release, repatriation and accommodation in neutral countries ((Geneva IV, Article 132; Protocol I, Article 76) and criminal sanctions (Protocol I, Article 76 (3); Protocol II, Article 6(4)). Further, during times of occupation, any

existing preferential rights of pregnant women and mothers of young children are to be respected (Geneva IV, Article 50).

122. Girls benefit from the protection of the general provision of international humanitarian law applicable to all victims of armed conflict, as well as the special protections available to women, and indirectly from the additional provisions protecting pregnant women and mothers of young children. Girls also fall under the protection of the special provisions of inter-national humanitarian law dealing with the protection of children. For example, Protocol I Additional to the Geneva Conventions provides that all children shall be the object of special respect and are to be protected against sexual assault.

123. The protection afforded by international humanitarian law is applicable in situations amounting to an "armed conflict". In general terms, an armed conflict exists when there is a resort to the use of force between two or more States, or protracted armed violence between governmental authorities and organized armed groups, or between such groups within a State. The determination of whether a violent confrontation within a State goes beyond the realms of domestic criminal law and can be categorized as armed conflict to which international humanitarian law applies can be difficult, especially when the State concerned indicates that it has the situation under control.

124. The legal consequences of characterizing a conflict as solely internal are significant, as Protocol II, which applies to internal conflicts provides fewer protections than the Geneva Conventions provide to those affected by inter-State armed conflict. Moreover, those protections do not apply in "situations of internal disturbances and tensions, such as riots, isolated and sporadic acts of violence and other acts of a similar nature" (Article 1, paragraph 2). Basic protections are also provided to civilians affected by non-international armed conflict through Article 3, common to the four Geneva Conventions of 1949. That Article prohibits violence to life and person, in particular murder of all kinds, mutilation, torture, cruel treatment and the taking of hostages, outrages upon personal dignity, in particular humiliating and degrading treatment and the passing of sentences and the carrying out of executions without previous judgement carried out by a regularly constituted court, affording judicial guarantees. In addition, where war crimes are concerned, although there have been important recent developments in this area as discussed in part B of this chapter, the Geneva Conventions create criminal liability only for those violations committed in international armed conflict.

125. Most conflicts which occur in the world today are non-international in nature. Although some reach the threshold of violence and organization required for the application of Protocol II, common Article 3 is perhaps the area of international humanitarian law most applicable to contemporary conflict.

126. International humanitarian law generally ceases to apply on the general close of military operations or on the final repatriation of protected persons.[2] In the case of an occupied territory, the Fourth Convention generally ceases to apply one year after the general close of military operations, but an occupying power which exercises effective control over a territory, continues to be bound by a significant part of the Convention for the duration of that occupation. A significant part of the conventional rules of international humanitarian law relating to conflict and occupation apply to "protected persons" only, that is, to persons who find themselves "in the hands of a Party to the conflict or Occupying Power of which they are not nationals".[3] The Fourth Geneva Convention, which deals with the protection of the civilian population, provides protection for the whole of the population of the countries in conflict.[4]

127. The protection provided by international humanitarian law to women and girls in times of armed conflict are complemented by those provided by international human rights law, with the Preamble to Protocol II to the Geneva Conventions recalling that international instruments relating to human rights offer a basic protection to the person. Human rights norms are particularly significant in the context of non-international armed conflicts where the protection provided by conventional international humanitarian law is more limited. Human rights obligations relating to the rights to life, to freedom from torture and other inhuman or degrading treatment, and to freedom from slavery provide legal protection against the majority of the worst abuses suffered by women and girls during armed conflicts. The International Covenant on Civil and Political Rights defines these rights as non-derogable, including in times of public emergency that threatens the life of a nation. International human rights law is fully applicable in the pre-conflict and post-conflict stages, where international humanitarian law does not apply.

128. The legal protection available under international human rights law, including those provided by the International Convention on the Elimination of All Forms of Racial Discrimination, the International Covenants on Civil and Political Rights and Economic, Social and Cultural Rights, the Convention against Torture and Other Cruel, Inhuman and Degrading Treatment and Punishment and the Convention on the Rights of the Child, apply to women and girls on the basis of non-discrimination. The 1979

Convention on the Elimination of All Forms of Discrimination against Women is the most comprehensive treaty on women's human rights, imposing legally binding obligations on States parties to end discrimination against women in the enjoyment of the full range of civil, political, economic, social and cultural rights. This Convention also expressly addresses issues, such as traffic in, and the exploitation of prostitution of women, which may occur in times of conflict or its aftermath. An Optional Protocol to the Convention, which entered into force in December 2000, enables individuals and groups of individuals who have fulfilled certain admissibility criteria, including exhausting domestic remedies, to submit petitions on violations of the rights in the Convention to the Committee on the Elimination of Discrimination against Women, the monitoring body established by the Convention. The Protocol also enables the Committee to initiate inquiries into situations of grave or systematic violations of the Convention in those States which have accepted this procedure.

129. Girls benefit from the specific protections for children set out in the almost universally accepted 1989 Convention on the Rights of the Child which are to be respected and ensured by States parties without discrimination of any kind, including on the basis of sex. By virtue of Article 38 of this Convention, States parties undertake to respect and ensure respect for rules of international humanitarian law applicable to them in armed conflicts which are relevant to the child, and to take all feasible measures to ensure protection and care of children who are affected by armed conflict. Further protections are provided by the Optional Protocol to the Convention on the Rights of the Child on the sale of children, child prostitution and child pornography, which provides detailed requirements for criminalization of these activities, and the Optional Protocol to the Convention on the Rights of the Child on the involvement of children in armed conflict, which seeks to limit the use of children in armed conflict, including through raising the minimum age of recruitment to 18 years. Both these treaties were adopted in 2000, and entered into force on 18 January and 12 February 2002, respectively.

130. A number of abuses associated with armed conflict or its aftermath, such as trafficking in women and girls, which have emerged as a particular concern in these contexts, are specifically addressed by international law. The first consolidated instrument on trafficking, the Convention for the Suppression of the Traffic in Persons and of the Exploitation of the Prostitution of Others was adopted by the General Assembly in 1950. Article 6 of the Convention on the Elimination of All Forms of Discrimination against

Women, and Articles 34 and 35 of the Convention on the Rights of the Child are also directed at the elimination of this abuse, while the International Labour Organization's 1999 Convention 182 on the Worst Forms of Child Labour requires each State party to take immediate and effective measures to prohibit and eliminate the worst forms of child labour, which include slavery, or practices similar to slavery, such as the sale and trafficking in children.

131. In 2000, the General Assembly adopted the United Nations Convention against Transnational Organized Crime, and its supplementary Protocols: the Protocol to Prevent, Suppress and Punish Trafficking in Persons, Especially Women and Children, and the Protocol against the Smuggling of Migrants by Land, Sea and Air. The Convention provides, among other things, for cooperation in investigation, mutual legal assistance, extradition where trafficking is concerned, while the Trafficking Protocol provides the first international definition of trafficking, and requires States parties to criminalize such activity and makes provision for assistance to and protection of victims of trafficking, and elaborates preventive measures and preserves existing rights, obligations and responsibilities with respect to refugees.

132. Responses by United Nations system organizations to address trafficking have included principles developed by OHCHR to ensure the integration of a human rights perspective into national, regional and international anti-trafficking laws, policies and interventions,[5] which require the human rights of trafficked persons to be at the centre of all efforts to prevent and combat trafficking and to protect, assist and provide redress to victims. The principles indicate that States have a responsibility under international law to act with due diligence to prevent trafficking, to investigate and prosecute traffickers and to assist and protect trafficked persons. They also make clear that anti-trafficking measures should not adversely affect the human rights and dignity of persons, in particular the rights of those who have been trafficked, of migrants, internally displaced persons, refugees and asylum-seekers.

B. Redress for women and girls for conflict-related abuses

133. At the international level, the main avenues of redress for women and girls who have experienced conflict-related abuses are through claims of war crimes, crimes against humanity and genocide. In some situations, such women and girls may also be able to claim financial compensation for their

war-related injuries. Legal developments during the last decade have focused on individual responsibility for abuses committed during armed conflict, with the Statutes of the two ad hoc Tribunals created by the Security Council to address crimes committed in the former Yugoslavia and Rwanda providing redress for victims through the international criminal law process. The Statute of the Special Court for Sierra Leone provides similar relief. The Rome Statute of the ICC, which recognizes that Court's competence with regard to war crimes committed in both international and non-international armed conflict provides world-wide jurisdiction to try individuals charged with the most serious crimes. Other extra-legal mechanisms have also been introduced to provide alternative, and in some cases, complementary avenues for redress. These include truth and reconciliation processes designed to address the violations of international humanitarian law and human rights law, which are intended to supplement traditional judicial proceedings. It is through these developments that the international community has sought to address the culture of impunity for violations in armed conflict, including gender-based violence, such as rape, enforced prostitution, and trafficking in armed conflict, with such violence being included within definitions of war crimes, crimes against humanity, and forming components of the crime of genocide, as well as torture or other cruel, inhuman and degrading treatment, and enslavement. Their goals are not only to deal with past atrocities, but also to form part of peace and reconciliation which is fundamental to nation-building or rebuilding.

War crimes

134. Those who commit war crimes incur individual criminal responsibility for their actions. The four Geneva Conventions of 1949 codify war crimes in provisions which identify "grave breaches", with each of the Conventions containing its own list of grave breaches, which are expanded by Additional Protocol I. Under the Conventions and the Protocols, States are obliged to look for those who commit grave breaches and prosecute them, or hand them over to a State willing to do so. States also undertake to enact the necessary legislation to provide effective penal sanctions for those who commit or order grave breaches.

135. Many of the abuses women and girls experience during armed conflict, such as wilful killing, torture or inhuman treatment, are classified as grave breaches of the Geneva Conventions and Additional Protocol I, but gender-specific abuses, such as sexual violence, are not expressly classified as grave breaches. Article 2 of the Statute of the International Criminal Tribunal to

address crimes committed in the former Yugoslavia (ICTY) States that Tribunal jurisdiction with respect to grave breaches of the four 1949 Geneva Conventions and Protocol I, including torture and inhuman treatment and wilfully causing great suffering or serious injury to body and health. Article 3 of the Statute also criminalizes violations of the laws and customs of war.

136. As a result of gender-sensitive prosecutorial policies, sexual violence has been charged under the Statute of the ICTY as a grave breach of the Fourth Geneva Convention relative to the Protection of Persons in Time of War in several cases. For example, in its 1998 *Celebici* decision, the Trial Chamber of the ICTY[6] considered whether rape constituted torture within the definition of a grave breach for the purposes of Article 2 of the Statute. In concluding that rape at the instigation of a public official or with such an official's acquiescence in situations of armed conflict was torture within the Statute, the Trial Chamber emphasized that gender discrimination was a prohibited purpose for the offence of torture.[7] Other decisions of the ICTY have also determined that rape constitutes torture within Articles 2 and 3 of its Statute.[8] Similar decisions have been reached by the ICTR,[9] as well as the Inter-American Court on Human Rights and the European Court of Human Rights.[10] In addition, the ICTY has determined sexual violence consisting of outrages on personal dignity, including rape, to constitute a violation of the laws and customs of war.[11]

137. Article 8 of the Rome Statute of the ICC defines war crimes as grave breaches of the 1949 Geneva Conventions. It also defines "[o]ther serious violations of the laws and customs applicable in international armed conflict..." as war crimes. Included within this list of crimes are gender-specific offences, namely: "rape, sexual slavery, enforced prostitution, forced pregnancy,[12] ... enforced sterilization, or any other form of sexual violence also constituting a grave breach of the Geneva Conventions". The crime of "committing outrages upon personal dignity, in particular humiliating and degrading treatment" is also included as a war crime.

138. Traditionally, war crimes were considered to arise from breaches of the law committed during international armed conflict only. Article 3 common to the 1949 Geneva Conventions, relating to non-international armed conflicts, is not included in the grave breach provisions of the Conventions, while Additional Protocol II Relating to the Protection of Victims of Non-International Armed Conflicts contains no provisions on grave breaches. However, recent State practice has established that certain breaches of the laws regulating non-international armed conflicts constitute war crimes, and they therefore attract individual criminal responsibility.

139. Article 4 of the Statute of the ICTR criminalizes "serious violations of Article 3 common to the Geneva Conventions and of Additional Protocol II", including "outrages upon personal dignity, in particular humiliating and degrading treatment, rape, enforced prostitution and any form of indecent assault". The ICTR has concluded that sexual violence constitutes a violation of the laws and customs of war[13] and has articulated the elements required to establish the crimes of "humiliating and degrading treatment", "rape", and "indecent assault".[14] Notably, in the absence of a commonly accepted definition of rape in international law, in its judgement in *Akayesu* in 1998, the ICTY defined rape as "a physical invasion of a sexual nature, committed on a person under circumstances that are coercive". It has also desscribed sexual violence, which includes rape, "as any act of a sexual nature that is committed on a person under circumstances that are coercive" and continued that "sexual violence is not limited to physical invasion of a human body and may include acts that do not involve penetration or physical contact".[15] In *Akayesu* itself, where evidence existed that girls were forced to perform gymnastics naked for the entertainment of soldiers, the Trial Chamber cited forced nudity as falling within the definition of sexual violence.

140. In the case of a non-international armed conflict the Rome Statute defines "war crimes" to include serious violations of Article 3 common to the Geneva Conventions. These include, "committing outrages upon personal dignity, including humiliating and degrading treatment".[16] In non-international armed conflicts "that take place in the territory of a State when there is protracted armed conflict between governmental authorities and organized armed groups or between such groups", the following acts are within the jurisdiction of the ICC: "[c]ommitting rape, sexual slavery, enforced prostitution, forced pregnancy ... enforced sterilization, and any other form of sexual violence also constituting a serious violation of Article 3 common to the four Geneva Conventions".[17]

141. Article 3 of the Statute of the Special Court for Sierra Leone establishes jurisdiction over serious violations of Article 3 common to the Geneva Conventions. These are defined to and include "outrages upon personal dignity, in particular humiliating and degrading treatment, rape, enforced prostitution and any form of indecent assault". The Statute also empowers the Court to prosecute those who have committed certain crimes under Sierra Leonean law, which include offences relating to the abuse of girls.[18]

Crimes against humanity

142. Like war crimes, crimes against humanity are also subject to universal jurisdiction and may therefore be tried by any State. Although long part of international customary law, Article 6 (c) of the Charter of the Inter-national Military Tribunal (Nuremberg Tribunal) provided the first definition of crimes against humanity in positive international law. Several indictments of the International Military Tribunal for the Far East included charges of sexual violence as crimes against humanity, but the Nuremberg Charter did not include gender-based crimes. The Statute of the ICTY includes gender-based and sexual violence expressly in its definition of crimes against humanity,[19] with Article 5 of the Statute of the ICTY conferring power on the Prosecutor to prosecute persons responsible for, inter alia, rape "when committed in armed conflict, whether international or internal in character, and directed against any civilian population". Article 3 of the Statute of the ICTR, which deals with crimes against humanity, also expressly includes rape.[20]

143. The Prosecutor has issued indictments in relation to both conflicts charging rape as a crime against humanity[21] and the Tribunals have found individuals guilty of crimes against humanity for, inter alia, rape.[22] Acts of sexual violence other than rape have also been charged as crimes against humanity, being categorized as inhumane acts, before both the ICTY and the ICTR.[23] The classification of "serious sexual assault" as a crime against humanity via the categorization of inhumane acts has also been confirmed by the ICTY.[24] Similarly "enslavement", another of the acts defined as a crime against humanity, has also been interpreted to reflect the perspective of women. The Trial Chamber of the ICTY in its *Foca* decision convicted defendants who had held women captive for sex and domestic service of crimes against humanity by way of sexual enslavement, thereby indicating that existing crimes are, increasingly, being interpreted to reflect the perspective of women.

144. The Statutes of both Tribunals and the Rome Statute provide that torture may constitute a crime against humanity if it is directed against any civilian population.[25] The Prosecutor has issued indictments against defendants before the ICTY for crimes against humanity on the basis of sexual violence as torture[26] and has successfully prosecuted sexual violence on political, racial and/or religious grounds as persecution constituting a crime against humanity.[27] The Rome Statute extends the range of gender-related crimes within the definition of crimes against humanity to include "rape, sexual slavery, enforced prostitution, forced pregnancy, enforced sterilization, or any other form of sexual violence of comparable gravity", provided these crimes are "committed as part of a widespread or systematic attack directed against any civilian population, with knowledge of the attack".[28] The Rome Statute further provides that the term "enslavement" means the exercise of any or all of the powers attaching to the right of ownership over a person, including the exercise of such power in the course of trafficking in persons, in particular women and children, thereby taking into account particular experiences of women. Accordingly, trafficking in women and children committed as part of a widespread or systematic attack directed against any civilian population meets the definition of a crime against humanity.[29] The Rome Statute also includes gender as one of the impermissible discriminatory grounds in the definition of the crime of persecution.[30]

145. The Statute for the Special Court for Sierra Leone is similar to that of the Rome Statute and includes within its definition of crimes against humanity in Article 2 "[r]ape, sexual slavery, enforced prostitution, forced pregnancy and any other form of sexual violence".

Genocide

146. The 1948 Convention on the Prevention and Punishment of the Crime of Genocide defines genocide, a term used in indictments of major war criminals at Nuremberg, as a specific example of the broader category of crimes against humanity. Genocide requires a physical act, such as killing, causing serious bodily or mental harm, deliberately inflicting con-ditions, calculated to bring about physical destruction, imposing measures intended to prevent births and forcibly transferring children. It is distinguished from other crimes against humanity, however, because a specific mental element is required: a specific intent to destroy a "national, ethnical, racial or religious group" in whole or in part. Although referring to the imposition of measures intended to prevent births within the group in Article II (d), the distinctive ways in which women and girls experience genocide are not expressly reflected in the Genocide Convention.[31]

147. Both the Statutes of the ICTY and the ICTR include genocide within the jurisdiction of the Tribunals.[32] In its *Akayesu* decision, the Trial Chamber of the ICTR found the defendant guilty of genocide in that he abetted the infliction of serious bodily and mental harm on members of the Tutsi group, through "acts of sexual violence, mutilations and rape", with the necessary intent to destroy the group in whole or in part.[33] The classifi-cation of sexual violence as geno-cide has been subsequently confirmed by the ICTR.[34]

148. It is to be noted that the definition of genocide in the Genocide Convention requires attacks on a "national, ethnical, racial or religious" group, and does not expressly cover the targeting of women solely on the basis of their sex. When women are specifically targeted, it is usually because they are within one of the specified groups and they are covered as constituting "part" of a group, within the meaning of Article II of the Genocide Convention. However, in cases where women are targeted for destruction solely on the basis of their sex, judgements of the ICTR provide support for the proposition that a flexible interpretation of genocide should be adopted.[35] For example, in the *Akayesu* decision, the Trial Chamber noted that the drafters of the Genocide Convention intended to include only "'stable' groups, constituted in a permanent fashion and membership of which is determined by birth, with the exclusion of more 'mobile' groups which one joins through individual voluntary commitment, such as political and economic groups".[36] In considering whether additional groups meeting this criterion might also be covered, the Chamber stated that "the intention of ... the Genocide Convention, ...was patently to ensure the protection of any stable and permanent group",[37] thereby providing support for the proposition that targeting women, exclusively on the basis of their sex, may fall within the existing definition of genocide.

149. Article 6 of the Rome Statute includes the crime of genocide within the jurisdiction of the Court, but does not make any specific reference to rape or sexual violence, adopting *verbatim* the definition of the crime con-tained in the Genocide Convention. However, the work of the Preparatory Commission of the ICC specifically acknowledges that, in certain circum-stances, sexual violence may fall within the definition of genocide, thereby confirming the approach of the ICTR in such cases as *Akayesu*.[38]

Rules and procedures for prosecuting international crimes committed during armed conflict

150. In addition to explicitly recognizing gender-based crimes, the constituent documents of the ICTY, the ICTR, the ICC and the Special Court for Sierra Leone include provisions to ensure the delivery of gender-sensitive justice. For example, the Statutes of both the ICTY and the ICTR provide for measures to protect the victim's identity [39] and the Rules of Procedure and Evidence of both Tribunals contain specific rules relating to evidentiary matters in cases of sexual assault.[40] A Victims and Witnesses Unit is also a feature of the Registry of both Tribunals. The aim of the Unit is to "recommend protective measures for victims and witnesses", and to "provide counseling and support for them, in particular in cases of rape and sexual assault".[41]

151. There is no requirement in the Statute of either Tribunal for gender balance in the composition of the Tribunals themselves, in the staff of the Registry or in the Office of the Prosecutor. The only exception is in the context of the Victims and Witnesses Unit of the Registry, where consideration must be given "to the employment of qualified women".[42]

152. The Rome Statute requires that in its "application and interpretation of law", the International Criminal Court "must be consistent with internationally recognized human rights, and be without any adverse distinction founded on grounds, such as [*inter alia*] gender, as defined in Article 7, paragraph 3 [of the Statute] …".[43] Provisions also seek to ensure that the Court has a balanced sex composition[44] and gender expertise in all three organs of the Court namely, the Office of the Prosecutor, the Registry and the members of the Court.[45] To provide protection for victims and witnesses, the Registrar is required to set up a Victims and Witnesses Unit.[46] Trials before the Court must be conducted with full respect for the rights of the accused, and with "due regard for the protection of victims and witnesses".[47] With that balance in mind, the Court is required to "take appropriate measures to protect the safety, physical and psychological well-being, dignity and privacy of victims and witnesses", and must have regard to, among other things, gender considerations, and "the nature of the crime, in particular, but not limited to, where the crime involves sexual or gender violence or violence against children".[48] Victims and witnesses also have the right to participate in the process at the ICC,[49] a development intended to give victims a more empowered role in the process.

C. Reparations for victims of conflict

153. There are several legal avenues for victims of armed conflict to pursue claims for compensation. First, compensation may be payable by a State that is in breach of its obligations under international law. It is a well-established principle of international law that a State must make reparation (which can include the payment of compensation) for its internationally wrongful acts. The United Nations Compensation Commission,[50] specifically recognized and compensated gender-based harms, such as sexual violence to women and girl children, injury to pregnant women, as well as other harms experienced by women, (albeit not exclusively), such as health effects of conflicts and certain types of economic loss.[51] Notably, the Commission acknowledged the difficulties associated with reporting sexual violence, particularly during times of armed conflict, and regarded all forms of sexual assault to be compensable, regardless of whether these acts were part of a widespread campaign of sexual violence.

154. Another possible source of compensation for victims of criminal acts during armed conflict are the perpetrators of the offence themselves. As the international community has assumed greater responsibility for prosecuting international crimes committed during armed conflict, this issue has received some attention. Neither the Statute of the ICTY nor of the ICTR expressly includes the power to order compensation as part of the penalties imposed on convicted persons, although both confer the power on the relevant Tribunal to order the return of property and proceeds acquired by criminal conduct.[52]

155. The Rome Statute includes a provision on reparation for victims, which can include restitution, compensation and rehabilitation which entitles the Court, either on request or its own motion to determine the scope and extent of any damage, loss and injury to, or in respect of victims. The provision does not explicitly refer to gender issues, although these might be taken into account by the Court when it establishes principles relating to reparations. Reparations can be ordered directly against a person convicted by the Court, and in appropriate circumstances, may be paid through the Trust Fund established for the benefit of victims of crimes within the jurisdiction of the Court, and their families.

D. Protecting refugee and internally displaced women and girls

156. International legal protection for refugees, IDPs and returnees, is provided by international human rights law, humanitarian law, and, increasingly, criminal law. Provisions within refugee law further strengthen the international legal regime protecting women and girls during times of armed conflict which are of particular significance in the aftermath of conflict. Policy directives and guidelines on the protection of refugee women, children and reproductive health, and against sexual violence, predominantly formulated by UNHCR over the past 15 years have led to the *de facto* expansion of protection for women and girls in this context.[53]

157. Under international law, the fundamental rights of refugees, returnees and internally displaced persons are essentially the same. Moreover, everyone within the territory or under the jurisdiction of a State has a right to the protection of, and is subject to, the laws of that country, regardless of migratory status, or sex.[54] Under the 1951 United Nations Convention relating to the Status of Refugees, those who meet the definition of a refugee in Article 1 (2) of that Convention, have access to a wide array of rights and protections, including legal aid and material protection, as well as the right not to be returned to the place where they face persecution. Successive conclusions of UNHCR's Executive Committee have emphasized the importance of gender-sensitive interpretation of the Convention definition,[55] and women and girls have been classified as refugees on the basis of gender-based persecution, including through sexual violence, and because they are at risk of severe discrimination as a result of transgressing social mores.

158. Persons who are internally displaced fall outside the framework of the Refugee Convention, but are protected by the international human rights framework, and, in many cases, international humanitarian law. While there is no international organization with the global mandate to protect or assist internally displaced people, a number of steps have been taken to address their needs. ICRC provides protection to civilians, including IDPs, in the context of armed conflict. Although UNHCR's governing Statute makes no reference to internally displaced persons, UNHCR increasingly provides assistance and protection to internally displaced persons on the basis of General Assembly resolutions and Article 9 of its Statute[56] when called upon to do so by the United Nations General Assembly, Security Council or Secretary-General. Nonetheless, the absence of internally displaced persons from its mandate prevents UNHCR from taking the initiative and planning long-term for the protection that this group of forced migrants requires.

159. The 1998 Guiding Principles on Internal Displacement, which are not legally binding, consist of 30 principles to provide protection and assistance throughout displacement and against arbitrary future displacement, and establish guidelines for safe return, resettlement and reintegration. These principles, which are based on the binding rules for the protection of IDPs found in international humanitarian law and human rights, seek to provide guidance to United Nations and international and national actors in working with internally displaced persons. They pay particular attention to the rights and needs of children, including prohibitions on the sale of children into marriage, sexual exploitation, forced labour and recruitment or use of children during hostilities. The principles also stress equal educational opportunities for girls.[57]

E. Challenges

160. A comprehensive legal framework exists at the international level to provide protection to women and girls during armed conflict and its aftermath, and this legal framework has been increasingly responsive to the experiences of women and girls in this context, in particular where sexual violence is concerned. The international criminalization of activities in non-international armed conflicts has been of great significance, as have gender-sensitive prosecutorial policies and procedural innovations that address the singular experiences of women and adolescent girls in the enforcement process. Another major advance has been the determination of command responsibility for many of the offences involving sexual violence against women and girls in armed conflict,[58] which has undermined the culture of impunity that previously pervaded in this context.

161. It is essential that these positive developments are maintained and further advanced. Although there is now a greater understanding of the use of sexual violence against women and girls in armed conflict, other important aspects of women's experience in this context must also be recognized and acknowledged adequately in the legal regime. Significant attention must also be paid to improving compliance with existing international norms. Steps must be taken to ensure that the requirements of international humanitarian and human rights law are widely known and applied, particularly at the national level. Here measures are required at international, regional and national levels to ensure that perpetrators are punished for violations of international standards in this area. Measures are also required to ensure that violations are prevented. This latter objective is affected significantly by the changed nature of armed conflict, with a large number of actors, including

non-State actors, private militias and children taking part as combatants. Many of these actors are unaware of the rules of international human rights, international humanitarian and international refugee law which provide minimum protection for women and girls in conflict, or if they are aware of these rules they disregard or openly flout them. In particular, many of these actors target civilians, including women and girls, often in gender-specific ways.

Recommendations

Action 1:   Condemn all violations of the human rights of women and girls in situations of armed conflict; take all necessary measures to bring to an end such violations; and call upon all parties involved in conflict to adhere at all times to their obligations under principles of international humanitarian law, human rights law and refugee law, in particular in regard to women and girls.

Action 2:   Prosecute all perpetrators of crimes of gender-based and sexual violence directed at women and girls in situations of armed conflict, including United Nations international and local personnel.

Action 3:   Ensure wide knowledge of international humanitarian and human rights law, including at the local level; disseminate information on the procedures for redress at domestic and international levels for violations of the rights of women and girls – such as ad hoc tribunals, human rights treaty bodies and all other relevant mechanisms – to the public in local languages, including to women's groups and NGOs; and take appropriate steps to ensure that individual women and girls, or others acting on their behalf, are not subjected to ill-treatment or intimidation as a consequence of accessing available domestic or international means of redress.

Action 4:   Take steps to ensure that women and girls, who are victims of gender-based and sexual violence and any other forms of violence during armed conflict, have the right to reparations for damages incurred.

Action 5:   Set targets for gender balance when appointing investigators, judges, prosecutors and other legal counsel to ad hoc tribunals and the International Criminal Court, as well as in the composition of truth and reconciliation commissions, human rights commissions, and other bodies; and ensure that judges and advisers appointed have expertise on such matters as violations of the rights of women and girls, including gender-based and sexual violence; ensure that prosecutors of such ad hoc international tribunals respect the interests and personal circumstances of women and girls victims and witnesses and take into account the nature of crimes involving gender-based and sexual violence and violence against children.

Action 6:   Ensure that national legal systems provide accessible and gender-sensitive redress for victims of armed conflict; that the mandates of domestic mechanisms of redress, such as truth and reconciliation commissions, human rights commissions, clearly reflect gender perspectives, respond to the needs, concerns and experiences of women and girl victims of armed conflict, and include special measures for victim and witness protection, especially of sexual crimes and violence; and ensure during all stages of trials or other redress procedures, measures to protect their safety, physical and psychological well-being, dignity and privacy, and gender-sensitive care and protection during fact-finding, investigations, trials and post-judgement periods.

Action 7:   Ensure that human rights components in peace-building and peacekeeping missions include, as a requirement for all staff, the capacity to address women's human rights and violations of international humanitarian law, human rights law and refugee law.

Action 8:   Ensure that amnesty provisions included in conflict settlement agreements reached under the auspices of the Security Council exclude from impunity all war crimes, and crimes against humanity and genocide, including gender-based crimes.

Action 9:   Ensure that judicial or quasi-judicial mechanisms that are established by the Security Council as part of conflict settlement arrangements interpret and apply the international legal framework relating to armed conflict and its aftermath in a consistent and gender-sensitive manner.

Action 10:   Ensure that all ad hoc tribunals created by the Security Council include judges and advisers with legal expertise on specific issues, such as violations of the rights of women and girls, including gender-based and sexual violence; ensure that prosecutors of such ad hoc international tribunals respect the interests and personal circumstances of women and girls victims and witnesses and take into account the nature of crimes involving gender-based violence, sexual violence and violence against children.

IV. Peace Processes

162. Peace processes consist of a complex range of informal and formal activities. Informal activities include peace marches and protests, inter-group dialogue, the promotion of inter-cultural tolerance and understanding and the empowerment of ordinary citizens in economic, social, cultural and political spheres. These activities are conducted by a range of actors, such as United Nations entities, international, regional, national and local organizations, and grass-roots organizations, including peace groups, women's groups, religious organizations and individuals.[1]

163. Formal peace processes generally include early warning, preventive diplomacy, conflict prevention, peacemaking, peace-building and global disarmament.[2] Activities include, inter alia, conflict resolution, peace negotiations, reconciliation, reconstruction of infrastructure and the provision of humanitarian aid. These activities are conducted by political leaders, the military, international organizations, such as the United Nations, regional and subregional organizations, such as the African Union (AU) (formerly the Organization for African Unity (OAU)), the Organization for Security and Co-operation in Europe (OSCE), the Organization of American States (OAS), the Economic Community of West African States (ECOWAS), as well as governmental, non-governmental and humanitarian organizations.

164. The participation of women and girls and the inclusion of gender perspectives in both formal and informal peace processes are crucial in the establishment of sustainable peace. Women cannot voice their concerns if they are not consulted by fact-finding missions or if they are not involved in peace negotiations. Political structures, economic institutions and security sectors negotiated in peace talks will not facilitate greater equality between women and men if gender dimensions are not considered in these discussions.

A. Involvement of women and girls in informal peace processes

165. At the global level, women have long been active in peace and disarmament issues. Individually and in groups, women have lobbied for the goal of disarmament. During the First World War, nearly 1,200 women from warring and neutral countries came together to protest against the conflict, and formed the Women's International League for Peace and Freedom

(WILPF), an organization that continues to advocate internationally for disarmament and human rights. Since then, women around the world have continued to pursue the goal of disarmament, including the total elimination of weapons of mass destruction, strengthened controls over the production and sale of conventional arms, the control of missiles, the need to reduce military expenditures and arms exports. For example, organized efforts by women – prompted by the discovery of strontium-90 in mother's milk and other radioactive hazards from the fall out from atmospheric nuclear tests – contributed to the conclusion of the Partial Test Ban Treaty in 1963. In the 1980s, a global women's peace movement spread across Europe, the United States of America, Canada and Australia with women's peace camps, established in at least 11 countries. In the Pacific, women organized against nuclear testing, and Japanese women set up a peace camp at the base of Mount Fuji.[3] Women's groups in Africa advocated for peace and reconstruction. Peace tents were a regular feature of the United Nations World Conferences on Women in Mexico, Copenhagen, Nairobi and Beijing.

166. The interest of women and girls in becoming involved in peace processes often stems from their experiences of armed conflict, whether primarily as victims or as armed participants. However, even those women and girls who voluntarily serve as combatants are normally excluded from the male-dominated political groups that make decisions during conflict and in peace processes.[4] Women and girls in conflict areas are aware of the potential for transformation and reform in periods of peacemaking and often work intensively to be part of this process.[5] It is important, however, not to generalize about "women" as not all women work for peace.

167. Involvement in peace processes can inspire or confirm in women an awareness of the political dimensions of conflicts and of their own political position. Women have identified working for peace as a unique opportunity to become organized, an experience that has proved useful in other aspects of post-war reconstruction. Women's peace movements often focus on the shared social experiences of women, thus producing greater solidarity across lines of division and making it harder to cast the enemy as an ethnic and dehumanized other, which is often a tactic of wartime propaganda. These opportunities for solidarity have been successfully utilized in Burundi, Cyprus, the former Yugoslavia and Sri Lanka.

168. Active involvement in informal or formal peace processes is a challenge for most local actors. It requires specific skills and access to resources and institutional support, which are difficult to access in conflict situations. Women and girls face additional constraints. Prevailing assumptions about

their appropriate roles in a society, particularly in relation to decision-making, and stereotypical assumptions about their areas of expertise, have been used to exclude them from informal and formal peace processes. At the Burundi peace talks, for example, some male delegates questioned the presence of women, seeing their wish to be involved as interference in the process in which the men represented them. In Guatemala, some men and women saw women's political mobilization as a direct threat to their culture and traditions. In Cyprus, the activities of local women activists were disapproved of, and women were told to stay at home and care for their children.[6]

169.   Local peace organizations may be resistant to the involvement of women. Male-dominated groups – even those devoted to peace – can reproduce assumptions about appropriate and inappropriate roles of women in society. In some cases, women may be invited to join existing peace groups, but can then be denied access to decision-making positions within the organizations, and relegated to "housekeeping" functions.[7]

170.   Assumptions about the role of women in society and conflict may also create opportunities for women and adolescent girls in peace processes. For example, women from the Democratic Republic of the Congo, Kenya, Liberia, Rwanda, Somalia, South Africa, Sri Lanka and the Sudan have drawn upon their moral authority as mothers, wives or daughters to call for an end to armed conflict. Women have organized as mothers, either to learn the fate of their children who have disappeared or to prevent their children from being conscripted or deployed to particular conflicts. Such groups include the Mothers and Grandmothers of the Plaza de Mayo in Argentina, the Mutual Support Group in Guatemala, the Group of Relatives of the Detained and Disappeared in Chile, the Association of Women of Srebrenica and the Committee of Russian Soldiers' Mothers in Chechnya.

171.   The concerns these groups have about their children give them a social legitimacy and a linkage with women from different sides of the conflict. Their identity as mothers sometimes, though not always, offers a degree of protection from official oppression.[8] The National Cooperation of Guatemalan Widows, for example, continues to campaign against the conscription of young men for a number of reasons, including the mothers' economic dependence on their sons. In Colombia, the mothers, wives and relatives of soldiers and policemen who were being held by the guerrillas have worked with both governmental agencies and guerilla groups to reach humanitarian agreements and, on occasion, have worked for the exchange of prisoners.

172.   It is often assumed that women and girls are not associated with violence during armed conflict, and as such they have enjoyed opportunities to

press for peace that were not available to their male counterparts who are seen as the planners, instigators and combatants. In some cases, women and girls have encountered fewer difficulties than men and boys in expressing their concerns about a conflict. For example, a women's march in Sierra Leone, in May 2000, set the stage for a march of parliamentarians and civil society organizations a few days later. Local observers noted that had it not been for the women's march demonstrating that peaceful expressions against the conflict were possible, the latter would have been impossible without inciting a violent reaction.

173.   Whether taking strategic advantage of prevailing stereotypes about themselves or becoming active in defiance of prevailing norms, women have proven to be creative and courageous participants in peace processes. An example is the role women played in Bougainville in the peace settlement between the secessionists and the Papua New Guinea Government. Women had been organizing networks of their local groups when the conflict broke out. They continued to organize in their own communities and to use their influence as intermediaries to the warring factions to keep a dialogue going across the conflict lines. They held peace marches, reconciliation ceremonies, prayer meetings, petitioned and led a protest against soldiers who were preventing the delivery of humanitarian aid. In 1991, they were able to create a "peace area" from which armed men were excluded.

174.   The opportunity to attend various national and international conferences gave impetus to the organizing activities of the women. The peace conference organized by the Papua New Guinea Government in 1994, the Fourth World Conference on Women in 1995, conferences subsequently facilitated by church groups and others held in Australia and New Zealand, gave the women an opportunity to discuss lasting solutions to the crisis in Bougainville. In a statement on peace at the signing of the Lincoln Agreement in January 1998, women insisted on being parties to all stages of the political process. As the signing of the final agreement drew closer, a Women's Summit, sponsored by the New Zealand Government, was held. Women set out their visions and proposed guidelines for the Government's responsibilities for women's affairs. Women stated their interest in greater participation in the new government and in political education to that end.

175.   Women are frequently active in reconciliation efforts. A Rwandan women's organization, the Women's Consultative Committee, is comprised of 95 separate associations. Of the 2,055 members, 60 per cent are widows of genocide victims and the other members are married to alleged killers who are in prison. Yet both groups work the fields together, prepare food for the wives to take to

husbands in jail, and stood together for election during local elections. As the Special Representative to Rwanda stated in paragraph 183 of his report: "Reconciliation of this kind is a lesson for the whole world. It belies the image of Rwanda as a country driven by ethnic hatred".[9]

176. Women have also used the media as part of peace processes, or to educate the public about armed conflict generally and its impact on women, adolescent girls, and girl children. In Croatia, the women's human rights and peace group B.a.B.e secured space for articles regarding peace and human rights for women in leading weekly magazines. In El Salvador, the radio programme "Buenos Tiempos Mujer", provided a space for dialogue between opposing groups to address violence in the family and society. In Guatemala, the publication of Rigoberta Menchu's autobiography, "I, Rigoberta", and the ensuing publicity campaign attracted international attention to the conflict between indigenous people and the military Government. In Burundi, the Centre for Women uses a series of media technologies to encourage and carry out inter-societal dialogue among women and their communities in an effort to strengthen women's work to resolve conflict and build peace.[10]

177. While a significant part of the organizing that women do in support of peace is related to health and reproductive services, the scope of these activities often extends to other areas that include advocacy and training in women's rights. The Medica Women's Therapy Centre, for example, which was established in Bosnia and Herzegovina in April 1993 to respond to women and children's psychological, gynecological and social needs that resulted from male abuse during the war, now also works on women's rights in the post-conflict era.

178. Women have also been involved in regional and international peace efforts. The Women's Peacemaker Programme of the International Fellowship of Reconciliation provides regional consultations that bring together women from different sides of conflicts for dialogue to deepen their understanding of conflict resolution and peace.[11] The African Women's Committee on Peace and Development, launched in 1999, and Femmes Africa Solidarité have focused on promoting conflict resolution in a number of African countries. Similarly, the Mano River Women's Peace Network brings together women from Guinea, Liberia and Sierra Leone. Women in Black, a women's peace network, that started in Israel, has inspired similar peace activities around the world, for example, in Cyprus and the former Yugoslavia. The tactic in all cases remains the same: women – usually from both

sides of a conflict – stand together in silent vigil as a way to proclaim to State and military leaders "you are not doing this in my name".[12] Another organization is Jerusalem Link comprising women from Israel and Palestine working for peace. Its representatives addressed Security Council members in an Arria Formula meeting in 2002.

B. Involvement of women and girls in formal peace processes

179. While there are many positive results of women's work for peace in informal peace processes, they are seldom included in formal peace processes. Women are usually not represented among decision-makers and military leaders, the usual participants in these process. As well, formal peace processes fail to take gender perspectives into account. Questions relating to differential impacts on women and men, the voices that are listened to, and the gathering of sex-disaggregated statistics are rarely part of these initiatives.

Early warning, conflict prevention and preventive diplomacy

180. Although the primary responsibility for conflict prevention rests with national Governments, civil society also plays an important role. The role of the United Nations and the international community is to support national efforts for conflict prevention and assist in building national capacity in this field. Despite the importance of these processes, there has been little attention to women's participation and gender differences and inequalities in these processes.[13]

181. Understanding the gender norms and customs of a society may prove useful in early-warning. At the beginning of a conflict, there is often a marked increase in militarism. There may be a corresponding increase in patriarchal values with intensification of nationalism that identifies men as the protectors of the nation and women as the bearers of the culture of the nation. The suspension of or restriction on women's enjoyment of their human rights often accompanies an increase in nationalism. There may be restrictions on inter-ethnic marriages or increased pro-natalism policies directed at women of one group.[14]

182. Indicators of impending conflict may include increased activity by women in food preparation. Farmers of both sexes, but especially women, may switch to planting short-cycle crops if a prolonged conflict is anticipated. Women may also become involved in the production of weapons, es-

pecially traditional ones, for purposes of defence or attack.[15] A detailed understanding of the society, the roles that women and men play, together with customs and norms associated with both male and female behaviour, is necessary to develop a comprehensive array of early-warning indicators of conflict for specific locales.

183. Conflict prevention requires a variety of approaches, including measures aimed at building mutual confidence, reducing perceptions of threat, eliminating the risk of surprise attack, discouraging competitive arms accumulation and creating an enabling environment for agreements on arms limitation and reduction, as well as on military expenditures. It encompasses both short-term and long-term political, diplomatic, humanitarian, human rights, developmental, institutional and other measures taken by the international community in cooperation with national and regional actors. The Secretary-General has observed that an essential element of conflict prevention is the strengthening of the rule of law, and within that the protection of women's human rights achieved through a focus on gender equality in constitutional, legislative, judicial and electoral reform.[16] The Secretary-General has recognized that to be effective preventive action must be initiated at the earliest possible stage of a conflict. One of its main aims is to address the deep-rooted socio-economic, cultural, environmental, institutional and other structural causes that underlie the immediate political symptoms of a conflict, and thus reinforce sustainable and equitable development activities.[17]

184. Preventive diplomacy is a process closely identified with conflict prevention. It aims to prevent disputes from arising, limit the escalation of existing disputes, and minimize the spread of conflict. Preventive diplomacy is performed by the Secretary-General personally, the Security Council or the General Assembly, or senior staff of the Secretariat, programmes and specialized agencies, and regional organizations in cooperation with the United Nations. Preventive diplomacy requires measures to create confidence, such as fact-finding and confidence-building missions, visits by Special Envoys to sensitive regions and analyses of early warning signs.[18] It may also involve preventive deployment of troops, and in some cases, establishment of demilitarized zones. Effective preventive diplomacy and conflict prevention requires the full commitment and inputs of all actors of civil society, including women's organizations.

185. Fact-finding is facilitated by soliciting information from all sectors of society, including women's groups and networks as well as individual women and girls. The appointment of more women as Special Representatives, Special Envoys and regional directors in peace missions may facilitate

networking with local women or women's groups. Currently, assessment missions focus almost exclusively on the activities of political parties and other formal political actors. Women are largely ignored because they may not be considered as serious political actors and are under-represented in this sphere. Discussions with women and girls and women's organizations would convey more details how conflict or emerging conflict affects people on the ground and provide information about the concerns that women may have. In the past two years the Security Council has made a point of meeting with women's groups during some of its assessment missions, such as in the Democratic Republic of the Congo, Kosovo and Sierra Leone.

186. Information provided by women is only useful if formal actors pay attention to what they are saying. Women report that the information they provide is frequently dismissed. In Liberia, for example, on several occasions, women reported a series of unusual movements of men and supplies on border waterways at night. The integrity of a woman Minister and the women informants was questioned and the information, which later proved to be accurate, was dismissed.[19]

Sanctions

187. Article 41 of the Charter of the United Nations provides that sanctions are one of the instruments the Security Council may use "to apply measures not involving the use of armed force in order to maintain or restore international peace and security". The increased use by the Security Council of this instrument has brought to light a number of difficulties, including unintended effects on vulnerable groups in the target country.[20] Sanctions can contribute to the suffering and death of civilians, particularly children; complicate the work of humanitarian agencies; conflict with development objectives; and do long-term damage to the productive capacity of the target country. Government, the target of the sanctions, tend to be the least affected. It is the most vulnerable groups, such as the elderly, children and the poor, who suffer as economies are destabilized, livelihoods destroyed, food and medical supplies reduced and electricity cut, affecting water, sanitation and health care infrastructure.[21]

188. There has been little analysis of sanctions from a gender perspective, but studies on the Persian Gulf War and the sanctions imposed on Iraq indicate that, due to the war, women increasingly became heads of households and primary income-earners. Whereas prior to the war and sanctions, households spent 50 per cent of their income on food, in the aftermath most

were spending nearly all their income on food for their families. As food prices increased sharply, many households suffered from malnutrition. Women and children throughout Iraq could obtain only two-thirds of their daily caloric needs. The workloads of urban women and adolescent girls increased as, with the destruction of infrastructure, they had to travel further to find food and water. Treatable diseases were left untreated due to shortage of medical supplies or electricity to preserve medicines. These factors resulted in 30 times more civilians dying in the aftermath of the war than during the war.[22]

189. The Security Council and the Secretary-General have called for efforts to fine-tune sanctions and measure their effects with a view to maximizing their political impact and minimizing their unintended negative consequences on civilians. Data disaggregated by sex and age is critical to ensure an adequate understanding of the gender-specific consequences of sanctions.

Peace negotiations and peace accords

190. Formal peace negotiations aim at achieving a settlement between the protagonists in a conflict, which are usually Governments, political parties, opposition groups, armies, warlords or militias.[23] Most negotiation processes exclude a significant number of actors, including women, who fall outside these official groups but who are equally affected by the conflict and are essential for building lasting peace.[24]

191. Women are under-represented in formal peace negotiations, whether as local participants representing warring factions, or as representatives of international authorities overseeing or mediating deliberations and institutions invited to the negotiating table. In addition, central issues of concern to women, including their participation in post-conflict political, social, civil, economic and judicial structures, do not always reach the negotiating table, in part because of the exclusion of women from the formal peace negotiations. Women not only call for issues specific to themselves but raise issues that affect society as a whole, such as land reform, access to loans and capacity-building. All actors committed to equality and non-discrimination – whether male or female – should have the responsibility and capacity to ensure that peace agreements incorporate gender equality issues.

192. Some women's groups, such as the Liberian Women's Initiative and the Northern Ireland Women's Coalition, have had success in including their proposals for peace and reconciliation in formal peace negotiations and plans. In Burundi, as a result of extensive advocacy, women were brought into the peace process, but only as observers because of the strong opposi-

tion from Burundian men. Yet, even as observers they were able to unite across ethnic, political and class backgrounds to develop a clear agenda, and almost all of their jointly-made recommendations were included in the Burundi Peace Agreement.[25] In Sierra Leone, women's groups actively participated in successive public consultations that preceded the signing of the Lomé Peace Accord in 1999.

193. In South Africa, women agreed across party lines that each party should have one-third women within the negotiating team for the formal constitutional process. This resulted in important gains for women. The South African Constitution includes a comprehensive Bill of Rights with provisions which prohibit discrimination on the basis of gender, sex, marital status or pregnancy; the right of women to make decisions about reproduction and control over their bodies; property rights; the right to health care, including reproductive health care; the right to education; and the right to enjoy and practice their own cultural and religious beliefs.

194. The opportunities for the involvement of women in formal peace negotiations and their capacity for effective participation are often dependent on their political mobilization prior to the peace process itself, as evidenced by the examples of Guatemala, Israel and Palestine, where women and adolescent girls were mobilized politically before the start of the formal peace process.[26] At the same time, however, women and adolescent girls who have traditionally been excluded from decision-making and peace processes can become more actively involved if they receive support from local and international actors. The Djibouti peace talks on Somalia, held from May to August 2000, included many members of civil society, including women, in the decision-making process at the conference. The presidium of six persons organizing the meeting included one woman; women served on decision-making committees; one woman served as vice-chairperson of the committee to draft the Charter. The efforts of these women resulted in an agreed allocation of 25 seats for women in a 245-member Parliament. The women described themselves as constituting the "Sixth Clan" and insisted that they should decide who occupied those 25 seats. At the end of the selection process, not only did women have their 25-seat allotment, some clans selected additional women in their own right.

195. In Afghanistan, the United Nations encouraged the parties to include women delegates in the peace negotiations. Women were full delegates in two of the four parties and advisers in the other two parties. The resulting Bonn Agreement contained an explicit commitment to the role of women in Government and created a Ministry of Women's Affairs. Two women were

appointed to the Interim Administration as Minister of Women's Affairs, and Minister of Health. The Afghan Human Rights Commission, which was established according to provisions of the Bonn Agreement, is also headed by a woman. The Bonn Agreement called for the participation of women in the Emergency Loya Jirga, a general assembly that would elect a transitional Government. In June 2002, about 200 Afghan women representing all regions took an active part in the Emergency Loya Jirga. The United Nations Assistance Mission for Afghanistan (UNAMA) in cooperation with the Ministry of Women's Affairs, provided them with training and daily support. Following the Loya Jirga, a network of 45 women delegates was created to play a leading role in women's preparations to the next Loya Jirga in 18 months.

196. Similarly in the Democratic Republic of the Congo, Congolese women from Government and rebel-controlled parts of the country gathered in Nairobi in February 2002, organized by Femmes Africa Solidarité and Women as Partners for Peace in Africa – Democratic Republic of the Congo, and issued a Nairobi Declaration and a Plan of Action to integrate gender perspectives in the peace process in the Democratic Republic of the Congo. The Plan of Action sets out goals, strategies and follow-up mechanisms for the incorporation of gender perspectives in the peace process, and the political, economic, social and human rights aspects of the reconstruction of the society. It also created Le Caucus des Femmes for the Inter-Congolese Dialogue, and called for the creation of a nationwide network to monitor violations of women's rights.

197. The political mobilizing by women in the Democratic Republic of the Congo prior to the formal peace talks made it possible for them to participate as delegates of political parties and experts from civil society in the Congolese peace talks, held in Sun City, South Africa, from 25 February to 19 April 2002. All political parties to the peace talks included women delegates, with 40 women and 307 men participating. Members of Le Caucus des Femmes participated and women were members of all five official working commissions. As a result of significant efforts, one woman was included in the commission on defence and security questions. The women acted as a unified dynamic force to keep the talks going throughout the frequent blockages in the negotiations, and formed parallel shadow commissions that met with all heads of delegations, international observers and the Special Representatives of the Secretary-General (SRSG). The United Nations Mission in the Democratic Republic of the Congo (MONUC) gender unit supported the efforts of civil society in the peace process, and Radio

Okapi (United Nations radio) served as a discussion forum to highlight the ideas and views of women throughout the peace process.

198. The systematic exclusion of women from official peace processes has detrimental effects on the long-term sustainability of a settlement because all voices and interests are not heard. In Bosnia and Herzegovina, even though the international community was aware of the violence and marginalization that women and girls had experienced during the conflict and the responsibilities they would be shouldering during the conflict and reconstruction, there were no women on the negotiation teams. In the Rambouillet negotiations prior to the Kosovo bombings only one woman was present, despite the active participation of women's organizations in the non-violent movement in Serbia.[27] In Colombia, the one woman involved in peace talks resigned from the process as a result of being harassed by other negotiators, guerillas and the press.

199. Women who are involved in negotiating peace agreements, are more likely to advance issues that are of importance to women and girls. The participation of women in the Guatemalan process, for example, resulted in specific commitments to women, such as access to housing, credit, land and other productive resources; the obligation of the Government to implement a national health programme for women and girls; commitments to reunite families and locate children and orphans; a review of the national legislation with the purpose of eradicating all forms of discrimination against women, and penalizing sexual harassment; a guarantee of the participation of women at all decision-making in local, regional and national bodies, on equal terms with men; and the creation of the National Women's Forum and the Office for the Defense of Indigenous Women, in order to promote women's participation and rights.[28]

200. However, the presence of women peace negotiators is not a guarantee that gender equality issues will be placed on the peace agenda. This was demonstrated in El Salvador, where although approximately 30 per cent of the Farabundo Marti National Liberation (FMLN) negotiators were women, gender equality was not included in the peace agreements.[29] The El Salvador peace agreements included discriminatory provisions in the accords, such as barring women to varying degrees from reconstruction programmes, with far-reaching consequences for adolescent girls, women and their dependants.[30]

201. If a peace agreement fails to note specifically the importance of gender equality, any measures proposed to promote gender equality in the im-

plementation phase can be interpreted as beyond the scope of the peace mandate. As analysis of the Dayton Peace Accords shows, provisions that are gender-neutral may create obstacles to achieving equality and non-discrimination in post-conflict situations. In its enumeration of rights, the Dayton Accords did mention the right to marry, but did not promote the inclusion of women in the highest levels of the new Government, with the result that from the beginning women were under-represented in Government and administrative and economic positions.[31]

202. Explicit attention to gender equality in peace agreements could include human rights provisions in new constitutions, implementation of special efforts to enable women's participation in elections, measures to promote the participation and involvement of women in decision-making, laws against sexual violence, and plans to prosecute perpetrators of gender-based violence. For example, women have demanded the provision of medical and social services to women and girls. The pursuit of gender-sensitive justice and land reform, protection against discrimination, and specific protections for poor, indigenous or ethnic minority women and girls are other central issues. Proposals to have a gender focus in development strategies, including in relation to access to credit and housing, inheritance rights, education and health programmes, including reproductive health, have also been sought by women activists in different countries.[32]

Peace-building

203. Peace-building is defined as "a means of preventing the outbreak, recurrence or continuation of armed conflict and therefore encompasses a wide range of political, developmental, humanitarian and human rights mechanisms".[33] A range of short-term or long-term actions can be adopted to meet the needs of societies falling into or emerging from conflict. To be successful, the process of peace-building should be locally owned and focused on social transformation and the re-establishment of trust through the participation of the national authorities as well as the local population, including women. The process should be designed to meet the specific needs of the country or region, and address the immediate security and humanitarian needs as well as the root causes of actual and potential crises.

204. Without specific attention to and understanding of gender relations and inequalities, women can be excluded from peace-building initiatives and as a result, their needs may not be met.[34] The incorporation of gender perspectives into peace-building efforts includes explicit support of both es-

tablished and nascent women's organizations working to become part of newly created political structures. It requires that international institutions working on peace-building are aware of the different priorities and resources of women and men, as well as boys and girls. Networking with women and women's organizations can facilitate mediation efforts, reconciliation and dialogue. Some women's organizations, such as the Mano River Women's Peace Network, have established sub-regional and regional contacts and expertise that can be drawn upon to provide information and facilitate capacity-building at regional and sub-regional levels.

C. Responses and challenges

205. Within the United Nations, the Department of Political Affairs (DPA) is the designated focal point for peace-building and has a mandate to identify potential or actual conflicts, to monitor political developments worldwide, and to provide early warning of impending conflicts and analyzes of options for preventive action.[35] In 1998, DPA established a Conflict Prevention Team to provide an intra-departmental forum for the development of preventive action options. Within DPA, desk officers develop country profiles on their respective countries and then monitor developments over time. DPA serves as the Convener of the Executive Committee on Peace and Security which was established in 1997 to deal with issues of system-wide preventive action. The Secretary-General's Special Adviser on Gender Issues and Advancement of Women is a member of this Committee. Other mechanisms within the United Nations system can also be brought to bear in early warning and conflict prevention, such as the reports of Special Rapporteurs and Representatives on human rights.

206. In 2001, DPA developed the United Nations Plan of Action on Peace-building[36] as a practical guide for the United Nations system in the formulation and implementation of peace-building strategies. Peace-building missions are meant to be temporary catalytic and facilitating mechanisms and are normally small. Currently there are four peace-building missions: the United Nations Peace-building Support Mission in Central African Republic (BONUCA); the United Nations Peace-building Support Office in Guinea-Bissau (UNOGBIS); the United Nations Peace-building Support Office in Liberia (UNOL) in Liberia and the United Nations Tajikistan Office of Peace-building (UNTOP). Their political responsibilities involve: protection of nascent democratic institutions; crisis management; political mediation; and provision of good offices.[37] These responsibilities are accomplished through provision of political facilitation and mediation; sup-

port to and facilitation of short-term mechanisms for reconciliation and dialogue; political, security and human rights reporting and monitoring; contribution to subregional and regional stability where appropriate and viable; advocacy and sensitization of national actors to human rights, security, democratic and peaceful means of conflict management and the rule of law; and advocacy and the dissemination of information on all aspects of peace-building.

207. As part of its peace-building efforts, DPA is sometimes involved in the political education of local elected representatives and in strengthening the role of local leaders. These activities can involve the training of women as voters and candidates for public office. An important element of human rights monitoring also includes monitoring violations of the human rights of women, as noted in the Plan of Action. This monitoring would indicate not only the extent to which latent violence may reappear, but also the extent to which new democratic institutions are taking root in the local population.

Informal peace processes

208. International organizations have not always recognized or capitalized on women's involvement in informal peace processes, since these are often small-scale initiatives concentrated at the local level. Public marches or cross-community development projects are not viewed as central to the peace process, even though they may be very effective in changing people's attitudes, opening up opportunities for more formal peace processes and acting as important catalysts for change. Women involved in informal peace processes may themselves not be focused on gaining the attention of official actors or intervening in the formal peace process. They often view their own activities as focused on questions of survival or equal rights, and may regard themselves as apolitical. One of the challenges for all international actors involved in formal peace processes is to become familiar with the variety of peace-related activism carried out by women at grass-roots level.

209. A challenge for those involved in informal peace processes is finding the momentum to continue their activism and involvement once the immediate goal of cessation of hostilities has been accomplished. Many groups of women who respond to conflict have larger agendas than peace alone, and their activism can generate multiple offshoot organizations. In other instances, once armed conflict ceases and people turn their attention to recovery, some organized efforts for peace-building simply dissipate.

210. Women involved in informal peace processes have identified lack of access to sources of funding as a major constraint to the achievement of their goals. Women's grass-roots organizations in situations of armed conflict receive little financial assistance from local or national actors, and many are largely dependent on international NGOs and international governmental and inter-governmental institutions.[38] Procedures for obtaining funding are complicated and protracted. There may also be conflicting priorities between donors and local groups. Women cite leadership training and skills training programmes, in such areas as peace education, trauma healing and counseling, as essential for carrying out their peace work.[39]

Formal peace processes

211. Women and women's groups involved in organizing for peace have identified the need to be included at all levels of decision-making of formal peace processes as critical to the achievement of their goals.[40] If the United Nations were to lead by example in terms of representation of women, local women would have a better chance of being included in formal peace processes.

212. One of the greatest challenges is harnessing the energy and activism that many women exhibit in informal activities and translating that into their participation and influence in formal activities. This challenge is intensified by the false assumption that peace processes are gender neutral, the negative attitudes of many participants in formal peace processes toward women's involvement and by the expectation that anyone engaged in formal peace processes should understand the manner in which they are conducted (including expectations of knowledge of international legal and other standards, United Nations protocols and terminology). Many women report that they need capacity-building opportunities to acquire the expertise required to participate in formal peace processes.

213. One way to support capacity-building would be to facilitate women's participation in non-official talks that are carried on discreetly at the level below the formal official process, and are referred to as Track II negotiations. Officials may be included, but generally the participants are people from all sides of the conflict in the community or the diaspora who have some influence in the community. Supported by a facilitator they discuss some of the main issues of the conflict and explore possible options for addressing them. The process helps to prepare the opposing sides for the formal process. The inclusion of women in Track II negotiations would give them the training and confidence to participate in formal peace talks.

214. In addition, many women who choose to participate in peace marches or reconciliation efforts may choose *not* to participate in formal peace mechanisms because it is unclear to them how such formal strategies will affect their lives.[41] Formal mechanisms, such as early warning may be carried out by international organizations, which are not always perceived as having the interests of local peoples in mind. Those involved in formal peace processes should devote more effort to public education campaigns that explain how early warning, peace negotiations and similar measures are not only important for formal political actors, but for civil society as a whole.

215. The paucity of information on the gender perspectives of formal peace processes is also problematic. While some work has been done on gender perspectives for early warning and peace negotiations, there are other important areas of the formal peace process for which little information is available at this time. For example, the potential impact of gender perspectives on preventive diplomacy or peace-building remains seriously underresearched. A comprehensive collection of data by DPA would be required on the ways in which the incorporation of gender perspectives affect formal peace processes. Research and analysis of peace processes, negotiations and sanctions regimes as well as reports to the Security Council need to fully integrate gender perspectives.

Initiatives by United Nations entities

216. United Nations agencies have been actively involved in efforts to promote and support women's activities in informal peace processes. There are a number of important initiatives aimed at increasing the participation of women within formal peace processes.

217. DPA, the Division for the Advancement of Women (DAW) and UNIFEM support women's groups and networks to foster dialogue conflict. This work is especially important for countries where the usual forums for discussion (newspapers, public forums, parliaments, etc.) are weakened or destroyed. Women's social and community networks may allow access to power holders and an opportunity to engage in dialogues in alternative forums. For example, in Guinea-Bissau, DPA's initial efforts to make contact with and bring leaders of the warring groups to the peace table failed. DPA then partnered with local women and women's organizations, which in turn made contact with leaders of warring parties through their own family ties. Through these efforts the leaders were eventually brought to the peace table.

218. A number of United Nations entities, including DAW, the Economic Commission for Africa (ECA), the United Nations Development Programme (UNDP) and UNIFEM, and regional organizations, have played a supporting role in a number of women's peace groups, including the Mano River Women's Peace Network, the African Women's Committee on Peace and Development and Femmes Africa Solidarité, by providing capacity-building in conflict resolution and negotiating skills. In addition, the work of the Mano River Women's Peace Network on conflict prevention, early warning and mediation has also been supported through provisions of funds to attend regional meetings and summits. This represents a positive start to working with regional and subregional organizations in support of the efforts of civil society and women's groups in early warning and conflict prevention.

219. In Burundi, prior to the All Party Women's Peace Conference, UNIFEM, in cooperation with the NGOs International Alert and Search for Common Ground, provided training in conflict resolution. This training served as an opportunity for dialogue and consultation among women from various backgrounds and ethnic groups, including women of the diaspora. Similarly, in 1999, UNIFEM began a three-year initiative to support women in Kosovo in integrating gender perspectives into ongoing peace-building activities. Working in close collaboration with OSCE, the European Union and United Nations departments and agencies, the project provides leadership skills to promote the active participation of women in the economic and institutional restructuring of the province.

220. In parallel with the Bonn talks on Afghanistan, two meetings were held in Brussels at the urging of Afghan women. The Afghan Women's Summit for Democracy was organized by international NGOs, such as Equality Now, in collaboration with the Office of the Special Adviser on Gender Issues and Advancement of Women and UNIFEM. The Government of Belgium and UNIFEM organized a roundtable on women's leadership in Afghanistan. The Summit concluded with the adoption of the Brussels Proclamation, which addresses women's demands with respect to the peace process and reconstruction of Afghanistan, including the right to vote, equal pay and equal access to health care, education and employment; the protection of women from forced underage marriages and sexual harassment; and the active participation of Afghan women lawyers in the drafting of a new constitution that would include principles of non-discrimination.

221. The Afghan Women's National Consultation, held in Kabul on 8 March 2002, was another effort to involve Afghan women in the long-term peace and reconstruction process. The meeting, which was organized by the

Ministry of Women's Affairs in cooperation with several United Nations agencies, adopted a plan of action that would guide ministries and international organizations on women's participation in the rehabilitation of the country as well as in all political and administrative processes. Under the leadership of the SRSG and the UNAMA Interim Gender Adviser, an Inter-Agency Network for Gender Equality was established. The Gender Adviser works closely with the Minister of Women's Affairs and considerable effort has gone into soliciting the views of women and facilitating their inclusion in the emerging political structures of Afghanistan.

222. The success of the peace initiatives of women's groups in Africa result from many factors. Women have recognized the value of focusing on cross-cutting issues of importance to them, and organizing across religious, ethnic and political lines. In several instances, women have organized locally but first used the opportunity of international meetings to express their views on political or peace issues. To allay fears that they were not suited to negotiations, they sought support from such bodies as Africa Women's Committee on Peace and Development and Femmes Africa Solidarité to obtain the necessary skills in conflict resolution at the community and regional levels. They have reached outside their national boundaries to make strategic alliances with regional groups and international organizations and NGOs, which could facilitate their participation in peace processes. In this way, they have put aside their differences, and made the sheer weight of their numbers felt in the peace process. They have understood the impact of unity, collective action and innovation and learned to use the media in different ways to effect change. Women interested in participating in peace processes have learned to build effective relationships and strategic partnerships with international and regional agencies, which could assist them with political and financial support.

Recommendations

Action 1:   Explicitly integrate gender perspectives into the terms of reference of Security Council visits and missions to countries and regions in conflict; brief Security Council members on the gender issues in the conflict situations concerned; include gender specialists in the teams wherever possible; maintain a database on gender specialists as well as women's groups and networks in countries and regions in conflict; and ensure consultation with these groups and networks.

Action 2:   Ensure that all peace accords brokered by the United Nations systematically and explicitly address the consequences of the impact of armed conflict on women and girls, their contributions to the peace processes and their needs and priorities in the post-conflict context.

Action 3:   Ensure full involvement of women in negotiations of peace agreements at national and international levels, including through provision of training for women and women's organizations on formal peace processes.

Action 4:   Systematically and explicitly address relevant gender perspectives in all Secretary-General's reports to the Security Council, and for that purpose, prepare and disseminate a guidance note on the integration of gender perspectives in reports of the Secretary-General to the Security Council.

Action 5:   Undertake analysis of the gender perspectives in conflict prevention and peace-building activities and ensure that all analyses of conflict prevention and peace-building, including negotiations, preventative diplomacy and sanctions, adequately reflect a gender perspectives.

Action 6:   Consult with civil society, including local and regional women's and youth groups, to ensure attention to the needs, concerns and experiences of women and girls throughout the peace process.

Action 7:   Identify women's informal peace-building initiatives and provide relevant technical and financial support and establish mechanisms to channel the outcomes of these initiatives into more formal peace processes, including through the involvement of women in Track II negotiations.

Action 8:   Increase access to information from women's groups and networks on indicators of impending conflict as a means to ensure effective gender-sensitive early warning mechanisms.

V. Peacekeeping Operations

223. In response to the increasing complexity of crises, peacekeeping operations deployed since the early 1990s have become multifaceted. Tasks assigned to United Nations peacekeepers are no longer limited to military activities and peacekeeping efforts are not directed only at parties to a conflict. Peacekeeping operations may include monitoring of human rights, police functions and the development of institutions supporting the rule of law. They may also include the creation of State administrative structures, assistance in the conduct of elections, the repatriation of refugees, mine action programmes, and the delivery of humanitarian aid.

224. Increasingly the United Nations is entering into partnerships with regional organizations perceived as having a comparative advantage for undertaking military or other specialized tasks. The United Nations has worked together with regional organizations, such as the North Atlantic Treaty Organization (NATO) in Bosnia and Herzegovina and Kosovo, and ECOWAS which has led regional military peacekeeping operations in Liberia, Central African Republic and Sierra Leone.

225. Peacekeeping operations have a profound impact on people's lives. Women and girls, together with men and boys, benefit from increased security and the continuation of a peace process. The impact of the peacekeeping operation can often be different for women and girls compared to men and boys. There is the potential for peacekeeping operations to have a positive impact on gender relations and inequalities. For example, initiatives supporting elections can facilitate women's participation as voters and as political representatives. Women and girls benefit when the peacekeeping operation is able to address and stop violence, including sexual violence. Civilian police elements of a peacekeeping mission may assist in the training, monitoring or restructuring of local law enforcement agencies and address violent crimes, including rape, domestic violence and other gender-based violence, such as trafficking in women and girls.

A. Gender perspectives in peacekeeping operations

Mandates

226. Few Security Council resolutions establishing the mandates of peace-keeping missions make explicit reference to women and girls, or the differential impact of armed conflict and post-conflict recovery on women and girls. None have included a commitment to gender equality as part of a mission's mandate. When women's issues are acknowledged, as in the case of Security Council resolution 1272 (1999) on East Timor, it is usually as an expression of concern about the impact of violence and large-scale displacement and relocation of civilians, including large numbers of women and children. Explicit reference is sometimes made to the impact of armed conflict on children. This is the case in resolution 1279 (1999) on the conflict in the Democratic Republic of the Congo and resolution 1181 (1998) on Sierra Leone, with the latter acknowledging the importance of establishing a more concerted and effective response to the needs of children in the context of post-conflict peace-building.

227. The mandate of a peacekeeping operation determines the nature and scope of the activities it will undertake. When the mandate is restricted to a specific military activity, as is the case of military observer missions, such as the United Nations Interim Force in Lebanon (UNIFIL) and the United Nations Military Observer Group in India and Pakistan (UNMOGIP), the possibility of influencing the wider political or social environment is limited. However, where the mandated tasks of peacekeeping operations include the monitoring of human rights or the establishment or restructuring of institutions, there is great potential for integrating gender perspectives into those activities. In East Timor and Kosovo, the United Nations missions served as transitional civil administrations, which allowed for special attention to the needs and concerns of women. In East Timor, for example, attention was given to gender perspectives in different activities of the peacekeeping operation and in the interim administration.

228. Mandates should make explicit commitments to gender equality, affirm the principles of gender mainstreaming and gender balance, make reference to the human rights framework, including the Convention on the Elimination of All Forms of Discrimination against Women (CEDAW), and highlight the importance of monitoring progress on these issues. Without clear, explicit wording on gender equality issues in mandates and adequate budgetary provisions, attention to gender perspectives in peacekeeping may

depend on the individual commitment of the head of mission and staff in different departments. Specific references to gender issues in the mandate of a peacekeeping operation can facilitate the integration of gender perspectives in all its substantive activities and can provide criteria by which to measure the performance of the mission in terms of its attention to gender equality.

Operations

229. Peacekeeping operations vary according to the specific mandates of their missions. A wide range of activities can be included, such as military and police activities; protecting and delivering humanitarian assistance; offering negotiation and good offices; strengthening the rule of law; training and restructuring of local police forces, monitoring human rights; voter education and other electoral assistance; and disarmament, demobilization and reintegration of ex-combatants.[1] Peacekeeping missions should investigate the gender perspectives in activities within their mandates.

230. In one of the most fundamental activities of peacekeeping operations – the establishment of security – it is important to consider that women and men may have different security priorities and needs; they may often relate to authority differently; and women may experience restrictions on their mobility. It is important that peacekeepers understand local dynamics and do not assume that all people have had the same experiences of conflict and post-conflict situations.

231. The activities of the civilian police component of a peacekeeping mission may include monitoring local police forces and training new or restructured forces. In the latter case, the objective is to create professional law enforcement agencies that adhere to international standards of democratic policing. Attention to recruitment and retention of women officers and community-based policing are other important issues to address. Expertise needs to be developed within new or restructured police forces to address gender-based crimes, including sexual assault and domestic violence during and after the conflict. This includes the capacity to work in a gender-sensitive manner with women witnesses and detainees as well as strategies to combat trafficking in human beings.

232. When peacekeeping operations include human rights monitoring, support for electoral processes, establishing civil administrations or promoting national reconciliation, it is crucial to both identify and address the gender perspectives in each area. In the conduct of elections, for example, it is

important for peacekeeping personnel to understand the norms and customs of a society prior to the election and determine whether there will be particular obstacles facing women in exercising their right to vote or to stand for office. Counteracting those obstacles is a prerequisite for conducting free and fair elections.

233. Peacekeeping operations can also benefit from consultations and links with local women's organizations, which are often sites of local expertise about service provision in the areas of education and health, including reproductive health, as was the case in the former Yugoslavia. Similarly, women's organizations can be important partners in the delivery of services, as well as in regard to the creation of political structures and holding of elections, as illustrated in East Timor.[2] This partnership can be facilitated by utilizing existing contacts with women's groups made by United Nations agencies and international NGOs.

234. Peacekeeping operations need to recognize that women and girls have also been combatants. The planning and implementation of disarmament, demobilization and reintegration programmes must identify and address the needs and priorities of both male and female ex-combatants and their dependants, as well as camp followers and others who had served in various support roles in the conflict. (For further discussion of this issue, see Chapter VIII.)

235. Peacekeeping missions need an effective public information capacity to explain their mandate to the population and to counter misinformation. This requires that information be provided to all groups, women as well as men. Information on opportunities for participation in new political and judicial structures, the progress of criminal and war crime investigations, including on gender-based violence and the kinds of services – economic, social, political and judicial – that may be provided through the peacekeeping mission is particularly important for women. The successful delivery of such information requires understanding the roles and responsibilities of women and men, as well as gender-specific norms and customs within the host society, and may be facilitated by contact with local women and their organizations.

Roles and responsibilities to promote gender mainstreaming

236. Missions that have made progress in promoting gender equality and women's rights have had the support of the highest levels of authority within the mission. The head of mission has the responsibility to promote

and facilitate attention to gender perspectives in all areas of work and demand accountability from managers and staff from all levels. A clear commitment to the promotion of gender equality in the entire mission is required from the inception of its mandate to its end. This commitment must be translated into concrete actions in all areas of the mission and should be the responsibility of all staff in the mission, particularly senior managers. The importance of gender perspectives can be reinforced in high-level meetings with political parties and consultative bodies, as well as through mission information activities in newspapers, radio and television programmes and posters.

237. One constraint to bringing attention to gender perspectives in peacekeeping missions is the fact that many managers and professional staff are still uncertain what relevant gender perspectives are in their areas of work and how they should integrate these perspectives in different areas of peacekeeping work. Peacekeeping missions therefore need to ensure that sufficient awareness and capacity to identify and address gender perspectives is developed among all staff. The concrete resources – such as guidelines, checklists, training programmes and standard operating procedures (SOPs) to help mainstream gender perspectives into the daily work of all mission components – being developed by the Department of Peacekeeping Operations (DPKO) should help to meet this need.

238. The ability of peacekeeping operations to fully integrate gender perspectives at the operational level is also hindered by the limited availability of human and financial resources at both headquarters and field mission levels. The importance of gender specialists and gender units to support management in fulfilling their gender mainstreaming responsibilities has been recognized. Their role is to promote, facilitate, support and monitor the incorporation of gender perspectives in peacekeeping operations.

239. At Headquarters, DPKO's Peacekeeping Best Practices Unit is the focal point for gender mainstreaming in the Department. The Unit currently lacks the human and financial resources necessary to effectively promote gender mainstreaming and provide backup to the field. There is no single person devoting full-time attention to gender mainstreaming. In June 2001, the Special Committee on Peacekeeping Operations recommended the establishment of a dedicated gender capacity for DPKO, which so far has not been approved.[3]

240. Gender advisers/units in missions need backstopping and support from Headquarters to be effective. This backstopping function could in-

clude the provision of gender-related training materials to field missions, sharing of good practices and lessons learned among missions, assistance in identifying potential candidates for gender posts in the field, and in the briefing and preparation of gender specialists going to the field, as well as the provision of guidance and advice, including experts and consultants.

Recruitment

241. Women's overall participation in peacekeeping operations as military observers, civilian police and civilian staff remains low. It should be noted, however, that the number of women in United Nations civilian police and military contingents is often in direct correlation with their low participation in national police and military forces.

242. Women have rarely been present at the highest decision-making levels in peacekeeping missions. The first female SRSG was appointed in 1992 to the United Nations Angola Verification Mission II (UNAVEM II). As of July 2002, there was one woman SRSG heading the United Nations Observer Mission in Georgia (UNOMIG) and there are women Deputy SRSGs in MONUC and UNOMIG. The General Assembly, the Security Council and the Commission on the Status of Women have drawn attention to this and the Report of the Panel on United Nations Peace Operations (2000), convened by the Secretary-General, also acknowledged the importance of ensuring fair gender distribution in recruitment efforts. [4]

243. Accurate supervision of adherence to peace agreements can be enhanced if peacekeeping mission personnel make contact and work with civil society, including women's organizations. [5] The presence of women within the mission may facilitate such contact and foster confidence and trust among the local population. [6]

244. International women in peacekeeping missions may act as role models for local women, especially in societies where women have traditionally played a secondary role. Local women, on the other hand, may be discouraged if they perceive that women and gender issues are being ignored and overlooked by the United Nations. It is important to note, however, that the presence of women is no guarantee that women's priorities and needs will be identified and addressed in peacekeeping activities. The gender mainstreaming strategy requires that all peacekeeping staff – both men and women – identify and address relevant gender perspectives in all activities in a mission.

B. Responses and challenges

245. The rapidly evolving environment of peacekeeping presents opportunities as well as challenges for the United Nations, especially in the promotion of women's rights in the post-conflict environment. A number of important efforts have been made and some significant successes and good practices achieved in incorporating gender perspectives into peacekeeping operations. A key advance was the 2000 Windhoek Declaration and Namibia Plan of Action on Mainstreaming a Gender Perspective in Multidimensional Peace Operations, which were the outcome documents of a seminar organized by the Lessons Learned Unit of DPKO and hosted by the Government of Namibia in May 2000.

246. At the same time, there are still many questions around the gender dimensions of peacekeeping and there is a need to better understand operational successes and failures. Concrete programmatic recommendations are needed for people working in every stage of peacekeeping. These recommendations can only come from evaluation of past experiences, consultations with women and men (inside and outside of peacekeeping missions), collection and analysis of sex-disaggregated data, documentation of good practices and ongoing analysis of gaps and constraints.

Training

247. A major challenge is assisting mission personnel to understand what gender mainstreaming means in every activity of a peacekeeping operation. Training is required to develop awareness, commitment and capacity of all personnel in peacekeeping missions on the relevant gender perspectives to be incorporated into their work.

248. Where sexual violence was used as a weapon of war during the conflict, staff in peacekeeping missions, that are mandated to do so, have a particular responsibility to be responsive[7] to the protection needs of women and girls and to investigate rape and other crimes of sexual violence, so as to end an atmosphere of impunity. In these situations, peacekeeping personnel – both women and men – will require specific training for their encounters with women and adolescent girls. In turn, civilian police should be able to train reconstructed or new police forces, as is the case in Bosnia and Herzegovina where the United Nations Mission to Bosnia and Herzegovina (UNMIBH) is training local law enforcement professionals to address domestic violence cases and trafficking in human beings.

249. DPKO is integrating gender perspectives into all training modules prepared for troop- and police-contributing States. The "Ten Rules: Code of Conduct for United Nations Peacekeepers", developed with the active involvement of Member States, is reiterated in all training materials and through mission-specific issuances on conduct and behaviour.

250. The Training and Evaluation Service (TES) of DPKO has developed an in-mission training package on "Gender and Peacekeeping". The objectives of the training programme, which is geared to both civilian and military/civilian police components, are to (i) inform peacekeepers of how the relationships between men and women and their gender roles and responsibilities are changed by the experience of conflict; (ii) to develop basic skills which will help peacekeepers recognize the different needs, capacities and expectations of women and men in the host population; and (iii) to make peacekeepers aware of the gender implications of their actions. It is expected that the Mission Training Cells will integrate the gender and peacekeeping package as a compulsory module into the induction training of new peacekeepers.

251. While the main responsibility for training should be in training units, field gender advisers can be important facilitators of gender training initiatives. In UNMIK, for example, the Office of Gender Affairs initiated training of departmental gender focal points on gender mainstreaming strategies, and in 2001, training of municipal staff regarding the mainstreaming of gender issues into all policies.[8]

252. During the first half of 2001, a consolidated training package was piloted in the United Nations Transitional Administration in East Timor (UNTAET) and in the United Nations Mission in Ethiopia and Eritrea (UNMEE). During the second half of 2001, training was undertaken in MONUC and the United Nations Assistance Mission in Sierra Leone (UNAMSIL). Currently, a "Gender and Peacekeeping" training publication is being prepared for use by Member States. With specific focus on conflict and post-conflict situations, the United Nations Institute for Training and Research (UNITAR), in collaboration with DPKO, has developed an initiative called "Training for civilian personnel in peacekeeping operations on the special needs of women and children in conflict". This training was delivered in UNMIBH in December 2001 and in UNMEE in June 2002. The same training, with an emphasis on gender considerations in the disarmament, demobilization and reintegration process, is scheduled to be delivered in November 2002 in MONUC.

ler advisers and gender units

Gender adviser positions and gender units/offices provide crucial sup-
to the heads of missions as they implement their responsibilities for in-
iorating gender perspectives into the work of the mission.

. If well resourced and strategically placed, these units/offices, led by
or-level policy advisers, can provide guidance to the head of mission for
nstreaming gender perspectives across the policy spectrum in the mis-
ı. They can liaise with the national women's ministry or office as well as
ıl society groups working on women's issues to ensure that the needs and
ıcerns of women are given due consideration in mission activities. Where
___ mission's mandate extends to institution-building relating to the rule of
law, they can advocate for the goal of gender equality and special measures
to ensure the increased participation of women in all fields.

255. Gender units were established in two large multi-dimensional peacekeeping missions, UNMIK and UNTAET in 1999. In 2002, with these missions moving from a phase of administration to a new phase of support to
local self-government, the gender units/offices were replaced by gender advisers, who continued to provide support to national efforts. A gender unit
was also established in MONUC. UNMIBH and UNAMA both have dedicated senior gender advisers. In UNAMSIL, a gender specialist works
within the Human Rights Section of the mission.

256. In East Timor, UNTAET established a Gender Affairs Unit to facilitate the integration of gender perspectives into the design, implementation,
monitoring and evaluation of all its programmes and policies. The Unit focused on building capacity and raising awareness through workshops and
training sessions and establishing networks for gender mainstreaming, both
within the mission and externally in East Timorese society. The Gender Affairs Unit raised awareness of the critical link between gender equality and
sustainable development and the need to take concrete actions towards the
goal of gender equality. The Unit defined its objectives and strategies on the
basis of the experiences and priorities raised by local women.

257. UNTAET's Gender Affairs Unit developed a knowledge base on gender issues by conducting gender analysis and gathering gender-sensitive
data/indicators to contribute to situational studies and general development
reports. As the mandate of UNTAET was to prepare East Timorese society
for self-government, the Gender Affairs Unit also undertook legislative
analysis in order to ensure that gender concerns were reflected in keeping
with international human rights standards on gender equality. UNTAET

provided a sustainable foundation for a future gender mainstreaming mechanism within the first independent East Timorese administration.

258. In Sierra Leone, UNAMSIL operates in an environment in which local women have been very active in the struggle to re-establish democracy and rule of law in their country. In close cooperation with other United Nations actors, the local human rights community and civil society organizations, the gender specialist gathers information on the human rights situation in Sierra Leone from a gender perspective and provides substantive information and advice on gender issues in the preparations for the Special Court and the Truth and Reconciliation Commission.

259. Gender advisers/units in the field do not always receive appropriate budgets to carry out their work, and must sometimes undertake fundraising to establish a functioning office. Some of the reluctance to approve resources for gender mainstreaming arises out of the very nature of peacekeeping financing, which is an assessed cost to Member States. However, leaving gender units to finance their activities through voluntary contributions diverts valuable staff resources from substantive activities to fundraising.

260. In the Democratic Republic of the Congo, MONUC in partnership with other United Nations agencies offers specialized training in gender issues to both civilian and military personnel who are involved in the disarmament, demobilization, repatriation, resettlement and reintegration processes.

Gender balance in recruitment

261. The primary challenge to achieving gender balance within peacekeeping operations includes the difficulties in obtaining a commitment of troops and personnel within a short period of time, as well as the significant under-representation of women within many national militaries and police forces. The United Nations often lacks the leverage to ensure that troop-contributing States provide more gender-balanced military or civilian police units. There is recognition within the United Nations that this is an unsatisfactory situation, and there has been a renewed appeal to contributing States to provide more women civilian police officers and military observers to serve in peacekeeping operations.

262. DPKO data show that women staff in peacekeeping operations are represented primarily in administration, legal and civil affairs and human resources management. The global staffing strategy for peacekeeping operations and the Galaxy recruitment system include a new Intranet/Internet-

particularly at decision-making levels. It is also true that more women than men may self-select against particular jobs and types of operations based on their familial responsibilities to dependants. In some contexts, women may also be excluded on the grounds that women should not be working in dangerous situations or on the assumption that host countries may not readily accept women in decision-making positions.

264. To address the selection of personnel for leadership positions in missions, the Secretary-General formed a Senior Appointments Group, comprising representatives of Departments and Offices of the Secretariat (DPA, DPKO, OCHA, OHCHR, the Office of Human Resources Management, the Special Adviser on Gender Issues and Advancement of Women and UNDP) to advise him. On behalf of the Group, DPKO maintains a central roster of candidates for leadership appointments to field missions. In May 2001, the Deputy Secretary-General invited Member States to submit names for inclusion in the roster, and asked specifically for the inclusion of qualified women candidates.[10] Previous requests have been made jointly by the Under-Secretary-General for Peacekeeping Operations and the Special Adviser on Gender Issues and Advancement of Women.

265. Since 2002, the Civilian Police Division of DPKO has refined its approach to recruitment of civilian police for service in United Nations field missions by interviewing each potential candidate individually. This provides potential for the Department to increase the number of women who will be deployed in peacekeeping operations, and also to recruit officers with specific expertise in issues, such as gender-based and sexual violence. Police expertise is needed to address trafficking in women and girls, with regard to investigations, appropriate punishment for perpetrators, and the provision of support for the women and girls who are trafficked.

266. UNMIBH is working toward establishing the institutional mechanisms to promote gender balance within a multi-ethnic police force, including recruiting more women. UNMIK's close cooperation with the Kosovo

Police Academy resulted in women being 20 per cent of the first graduating class. These women are deployed throughout the provinces and perform the range of policing tasks, thus visibly contributing to institution-building and reconstruction. Another example to illustrate the importance of integrating gender perspectives into security sector reform processes is the work done in UNTAET's civilian police component with regard to the representation of women and capacity-building in the local police force.

Standards of conduct

267. All personnel of a United Nations peacekeeping or other field mission are expected to observe high standards of conduct. Civilian staff are bound by the United Nations Staff Regulations and Rules and other relevant administrative issuances. Article 101, paragraph 3, of the Charter of the United Nations places an affirmative obligation on staff to uphold the highest standards of integrity. The standards of conduct for the international civil service which were adopted in 2001 by the International Civil Service Commission to replace the 1954 Report from the International Civil Service Advisory Board, while not having the force of law, provide an important overview of the standards of conduct expected from United Nations staff. The Peacekeepers Code of Conduct notes explicitly that peacekeepers should not "indulge in immoral acts of sexual, physical or psychological abuse or exploitation of the local population or United Nations staff, especially women and children".[11]

268. There is some evidence that prostitution increases with international intervention. In some instances, peacekeeping personnel may have condoned the establishment of brothels and been complicit in the trafficking in women and girls.[12] There have been situations where male peacekeepers engaged women and girls in relationships, including "fake marriages", which lasted for the duration of the peacekeepers' deployment. Children born of such unions are often left to be raised by their mothers after the peacekeepers return to their home countries.[13] In addition, as reported in Cambodia, Kosovo, Mozambique, and Somalia some male peacekeeping personnel have been accused of harassing and physically and sexually assaulting women and girls.[14]

269. It is necessary to ensure that the sexual harassment, exploitation or assault of local women and girls does not occur, particularly by personnel associated with the United Nations.

270. DPKO is reviewing and improving its procedures on disciplinary matters, and has requested missions to improve monitoring mechanisms, to ensure that appropriate action is taken. All missions have clear instructions to thoroughly investigate any allegation of sexual exploitation or assault by any peacekeeping personnel and to ensure that offenders are duly disciplined.

271. An active dialogue is being pursued with Member States to ensure that such violations do not occur. The status-of-forces agreements signed between the United Nations and a country hosting a peacekeeping operation, and the memorandum of understanding concluded between the United Nations and a contributing State, accord exclusive jurisdiction to the contributing State in the event that a military member of a peacekeeping mission commits a crime.[15] However, too often, contributing States fail to prosecute their nationals accused of serious wrongdoing while on service for the United Nations. Sometimes, a contributing State may not even follow-up on an accusation. Angry local reaction to the apparent impunity of illegal acts committed by international personnel has been recorded in a number of countries hosting peacekeeping missions.

272. Strong leadership statements about the need for the highest standards of behaviour at all times, coupled with setting an example of appropriate behaviour, are required of all mission senior managers. Some missions have instituted strict off-limits policies for their personnel and conduct regular monitoring of after-hours "rest and relaxation" venues. Other useful strategies that are being shared among missions include monitoring mechanisms set up jointly with local community groups and the establishment of ombudsman offices in missions.

Strategies for capacity-building to support women's participation

273. One of the most common demands made by women in transition to post-conflict situations is for assistance in enhancing their involvement in elections and public political activity.

274. During the UNTAC mission, which involved conducting the first democratic election in Cambodia, UNTAC Radio offered a daily segment on the difficulties faced by women in Cambodia generally, and their impact on women's ability to vote in the upcoming general elections. The Women's Summit brought together Cambodian women from all sectors of society to identify and prioritize women's issues in order to lobby political parties contesting the election.

275. These efforts were successful in getting a large proportion of the female electorate to participate in the May 1993 elections, and were also credited with encouraging the emergence of an indigenous women's movement in Cambodia. Support was directed to existing indigenous women's NGOs and to the creation of some new women's NGOs. These NGOs, in turn, mounted an effective lobby of the Cambodian Government so that provisions on equality were eventually included in the new Cambodian Constitution. Encouragement and support for women's political activism helped establish that women's participation in politics, broadly defined, was both legitimate and useful.

276. The missions in East Timor and Kosovo also actively supported the increased participation of women in governmental and administrative structures. Through workshops and training sessions they helped prepare potential candidates in the technical and political aspects of running for office. In Kosovo, important strategies by the mission included increasing the participation of women in key administrative structures, such as the Kosovo Joint Interim Administrative Structure and the Kosovo Transitional Council, and supporting the participation of women in the post-conflict planning process. Under the regulations governing the first Kosovo general elections of November 2001, UNMIK set a minimum percentage for women candidates in all political parties and stipulated that if a member resigned from the Kosovo Assembly, the replacement must be of the same sex. This resulted in a 28 per cent representation by women in the Kosovo Assembly. The mission also assisted potential women candidates through training and capacity-building workshops that familiarized them with the political process and the technical aspects of running for office.

277. The capacity-building provided by Radio UNTAET in broadcasts and workshops for potential candidates prior to the elections for the National Constituent Assembly facilitated the election of 27 per cent women to the Assembly. In addition to quotas, other affirmative action measures included extra airtime on United Nations broadcast facilities for female candidates, support networks that allowed potential women candidates to participate in training workshops, encouragement to women's civil society groups to support women candidates and high-level advocacy for the inclusion of women's concerns in party platforms. UNIFEM provided support for these activities. Due, in part, to the consciousness raising by UNTAET around gender equality and non-discrimination, the Constitution of East Timor of March 2002 includes the objectives "to promote and guarantee the effective equality of opportunities between women and men" and the principle of non-discrimination on grounds of gender.

Addressing violence against women and girls and trafficking

278. A number of peacekeeping operations have taken steps to address violence against women and girls and trafficking. Activities include a variety of measures, such as public awareness campaigns, training of the local police, supporting local organizations and developing special mechanisms within local law enforcement structures.

279. In Kosovo, UNMIK police introduced a domestic violence policy in September 2000, which provides direction to all officers on how to respond to incidents of domestic violence. The policy establishes the duties of the regional domestic violence coordinators, who are present in all regional police headquarters. Domestic violence training is also provided by UNMIK to trainees at the Kosovo Police Service School.

280. Development of public awareness of the problem of domestic violence is another good practice example. In conjunction with the UNTAET Gender Affairs Unit, UNFPA established a two-year programme addressing domestic violence, a priority area highlighted by East Timorese women. A major nation-wide campaign was launched in February 2002, involving posters, public service announcements and using all media. The purpose was to raise awareness on prevention of domestic violence and to provide information on available assistance. The mission helped train local journalists on gender-sensitive reporting of such crimes. The campaign mobilized church and political leaders, as well as law enforcement officials and the media to create messages urging an end to such acts. An East Timorese Government task force has been established with police, health, social services, United Nations agencies and human rights bodies to examine ways of addressing the issue in government policies and programmes. UNTAET civilian police established a Vulnerable People's Unit staffed by women to handle cases of gender-based violence. While it was established first in the capital Dili, district units are being set up across East Timor.

281. In MONUC, the respect for the human rights of women is being addressed by the human rights components of the mission. Human rights officers have recorded several cases of rape and have recommended the establishment of outreach programmes for rape victims. Human rights officers have also assisted in the release of female prisoners who were being detained for charges, such as adultery, which only applied to women.

282. In Georgia, UNOMIG through its human rights office in Abkhazia has supported the initiatives of local and international civil society organizations as well as intergovernmental organizations working to build the ca-

pacities of local women's groups for national reconciliation and peace-building. The human rights office has been working to publicize women's rights in its interactions with local law enforcement agencies, the mass media and representatives of institutions of higher education.

283. In order to tackle the growing number of cases of trafficking in women, UNMIBH, in close cooperation with OHCHR, established a programme called the Special Trafficking Operations Programme (STOP). The functions of the STOP teams include: updating lists of suspected locations of trafficking victims; monitoring raids and inspections by local police; interviewing possible victims of trafficking to identify their status and provide assistance on their request; monitoring local criminal investigations into trafficking cases and following progress through the judicial process (in coordination with other international agencies); and ensuring appropriate investigations into allegations of local police involvement in trafficking. STOP teams provide a point of contact for local citizens and former nightclub employees wishing to give information on trafficking. Information gathered from investigations and informal sources help identify suspected premises where trafficked women could be held and build cases for prosecution against those directly involved in these activities. Mechanisms for assistance also include regular cooperation with IOM on repatriation issues.

284. In Kosovo, UNMIK promulgated a regulation "On the Prohibition of Trafficking in Persons in Kosovo", which makes human trafficking a criminal offence punishable by sentences from 2 to 20 years, while also providing better protection for and assistance to victims. An Information Circular currently under revision details the responsibility of UNMIK personnel for complying with this regulation as well as the implications for non-compliance. A Victims Advocacy and Assistance Unit in the Department of Justice coordinates a comprehensive assistance and advocacy policy for victims.

285. In October 2000, UNMIK police gave priority to trafficking and established five regional units which focused on developing information on trafficking cases, women working in these circumstances and the establishments where such activities are occurring. These units also determine parties responsible and gather substantive evidence for successful prosecution in the courts. UNMIK civilian police also issue a monthly list of "off-limits" premises for UNMIK personnel.

286. The challenge for future peacekeeping operations will be to shift the focus from dealing with the existing problem to the prevention of traffick-

ing. International police officers with skills in these areas need to be deployed to train new or restructured police forces.

Recommendations

Action 1: Incorporate gender perspectives explicitly into mandates of all peacekeeping missions, including provisions for monitoring and reporting violations of international law as they pertain to women to the Security Council.

Action 2: Increase responsiveness to the protection needs of women and girls; investigate gender-based and sexual violence; and end impunity regarding violations of the human rights of women and girls.

Action 3: Consult with civil society, including local women's groups and networks, to ensure collection of information from all stakeholders and attention to the specific needs, concerns and experiences of women and girls in the implementation of peacekeeping operations.

Action 4: Systematically and explicitly address gender perspectives in all Secretary-General's reports on peacekeeping missions to the Security Council, and for that purpose, prepare and disseminate a guidance note on the integration of gender perspectives in reports of the Secretary-General to the Security Council.

Action 5: Ensure that peacekeeping operations have adequate capacity for fact-finding and reporting on gender-specific violations of the rights of women and girls under international humanitarian law and human rights law, including through the provision of training on culturally appropriate interview techniques and trauma counselling and the use of female personnel (such as protection officers, medical personnel, and interpreters).

Action 6: Review and strengthen codes of conduct to ensure that expected standards of conduct to prevent sexual exploitation and abuse of women and girls are clearly defined; disseminate the codes of conduct, including through training, to all personnel in peace operations – both before and during deployment; rigorously enforce these codes of conduct; and make public the accountability and disciplinary measures which apply to

United Nations personnel in the event of a breach of the standards of conduct.

Action 7: Disseminate information on standards of conduct in peacekeeping operations and ensure that troop contributing countries adhere to existing policies and codes of conduct of the United Nations on gender equality, particularly relating to sexual exploitation of women and girls, and put in place adequate accountability mechanisms and disciplinary measures.

Action 8: Review standard operating procedures, instructions, guidelines and manuals used to guide operational activities and incorporate gender perspectives.

Action 9: Monitor and report on gender issues in peacekeeping, including on all forms of violence against women and girls, as an integral part of mission reporting.

Action 10: Require that all data collected in research, assessments and appraisals, monitoring and evaluation and reporting on peace operations is systematically disaggregated by sex and age and that specific data on the situation of women and girls and the impact of interventions on them is provided.

Action 11: Set concrete targets for the appointment of women as Special Representatives and Special Envoys of the Secretary-General.

Action 12: Increase the recruitment of women as military observers, peacekeeping troops, and civilian police by troop contributing countries.

Action 13: Ensure necessary financial and human resources for gender mainstreaming, including for capacity-building activities, as well as for targeted projects for women and girls, as part of approved mission budgets.

Action 14: Establish awareness of and capacity to address gender issues as a standard professional requirement for all senior staff in peace operations, for example, Special Representatives of the Secretary-General, Force Commanders, Chief Administrative Officers, Special Envoys and peace negotiators; clearly incorporate responsibilities for promoting gender equality into the job descriptions of senior staff, including SRSGs; and require regular reporting on gender mainstreaming.

Action 15: Create the post of a Senior Gender Adviser at Headquarters in the Department of Peacekeeping Operations, reporting to the Under-Secretary-General, to support mainstreaming of gender perspectives in all departmental activities at Headquarters as well as provide adequate backstopping to field operations.

Action 16: Appoint gender advisers/gender focal points in missions with complex, multi-faceted mandates to support the work of the Special Representatives of the Secretary-General on incorporation of gender perspectives throughout the work of peacekeeping missions; and give adequate attention to location, mandates, resources, reporting lines and support from top management, as well as systematic backstopping from Headquarters, of these positions.

Action 17: Ensure that training for all personnel in peacekeeping operations – military, police and civilian staff – both before and during deployment, adequately addresses the issue of violence against women, including domestic violence and trafficking, within a human rights framework.

Action 18: Provide adequate training on gender perspectives to all international and local peacekeeping personnel – before and during deployment.

Action 19: Develop and disseminate training of trainer programmes on gender perspectives in peacekeeping operations to support national and regional training initiatives for military and police prior to deployment.

VI. Humanitarian Operations

287.   Changes in the political landscape during the 1990s significantly altered the goals and working methods of international aid agencies, in particular those working in countries affected by armed conflict. The recent move from channeling relief primarily through State agencies, especially in countries affected by armed conflict, to other channels is perhaps the first systematic response by the international aid system to violence resulting from governance crises in States. This shift has led to the development of more extensive ties with international NGOs and, in some cases, the privatization of humanitarian aid and relief, as in the Sudan after 1989. In the early 1990s, military force was used in some cases to secure humanitarian access where, it was argued, negotiation had failed. In Bosnia and Herzegovina, northern Iraq, Rwanda and Somalia, armed forces, usually under the United Nations flag, were deployed primarily to protect humanitarian relief agencies and workers.1 The participation of regional organizations in responding to situations of armed conflict and post-conflict also increased during the 1990s.

288.   While in the past United Nations departments and agencies tended to work independently of each other, today's complex humanitarian emergencies require continuous and improved coordination and cooperation among them. OCHA is mandated to coordinate the responses of aid agencies in emergency situations. The head of the Office chairs the Executive Committee on Humanitarian Affairs (ECHA) and facilitates the implementation of tasks, which are performed by various operational departments and agencies.

289.   Activities undertaken by United Nations humanitarian agencies in conflict or post-conflict situations are multiple and complex. They address the welfare of those affected by conflict, including of refugees, displaced persons and ex-combatants. Humanitarian agencies play a central role in facilitating the flow of international aid or, in situations where Governments are not yet established, taking the lead in managing incoming international aid. Agencies may also work with Governments to develop appropriate approaches to demining, including policy guidance, technical assistance and fund-raising for mine removal. In general, while humanitarian agencies also take the lead in quick-impact, small-scale projects, such as rebuilding schools, health clinics, roads, bridges and wells, longer-term development projects in post-conflict situations are undertaken by United Nations agen-

cies focused on development in an approach that aims at integrating relief, rehabilitation and development objectives.

290. Development agencies within the United Nations system and international, regional and national development agencies are increasingly active in conflict and post-conflict situations. The main activities of such agencies include longer-term strengthening of the public and social sectors including the promotion of effective and accountable public institutions and policy frameworks, building civil society, and provision and re-establishment of basic health care, education and clean water systems. Development agencies provide emergency transport, communication services, relief supplies and technical assistance for countries affected by crises and conflict. In addition, they assist in first time general elections providing assistance to national governments for future elections and strengthening and re-establishing national government systems at many levels. They also provide support to creating an operative judiciary, including providing legal advice and training judicial personnel, re-equipping courts and legal offices, and improving conditions in jails and prisons, and training of civilian prison guards. Given the many ways in which humanitarian and development concerns interact and affect one another, and given the long-lasting social and economic impacts of conflicts, it is critical to ensure that gender-perspectives are systematically integrated into the full range of emergency and development operations.

291. In humanitarian efforts, the United Nations departments and specialized agencies, funds and programmes collaborate with organizations, such as the ICRC, the International Federation of Red Cross and Red Crescent Societies (IFRC), IOM and several hundred NGOs, as well as with bilateral aid agencies. While military and police components operating under the United Nations focus on issues of protection and security, the humanitarian agencies are engaged in a variety of protection, assistance and relief measures, including meeting people's immediate and basic needs for shelter, food, water, sanitary living conditions, and medical care.[2]

A. Gender perspectives in humanitarian operations

292. Many of the specific experiences and needs of women discussed in Chapter II on the impact of armed conflict on women and girls continue during humanitarian and emergency situations and operations. The analysis of the gender perspectives in refugee and displacement situations given earlier in this study also applies and, therefore, only the most salient issues are presented. A synopsis of the re-

sponses and challenges of the humanitarian community in addressing these experiences and needs is provided.

Protection issues and prevention of violence

293. With civilians comprising the primary targets and victims, it is increasingly important that humanitarian operations further develop and strengthen their protection mechanisms. While protection is part of the mandates of many of the humanitarian agencies, and protection issues are increasingly being mainstreamed throughout the United Nations responses to armed conflict,[3] there is no commonly agreed operational definition of minimum standards of protection.

294. The State is the entity primarily responsible for protection of civilians, with international efforts providing complementary or supplemental support. Where the State cannot or will not protect its civilian populations, the international community has, at times, taken on the responsibility to provide that protection. Regional organizations, including the Council of Europe, AU (formerly OAU) ECOWAS, OAS, OSCE, the Southern African Development Community (SADC) and the League of Arab States, have worked with the United Nations. Civil society actors, including NGOs, have also demonstrated that they can exert considerable influence on public policy and encourage respect for international law, in particular human rights and humanitarian law. These groups are often the first to document and bring to the attention of the international community violations of international humanitarian law and human rights, and the humanitarian situation in conflict zones. The private sector can also play an important role in complementing humanitarian efforts in areas where humanitarian organizations were at times unwilling or unable to work, as in the Sudan, where private livestock pharmacists have worked to maintain supplies of emergency livestock medicines in conflict- and drought-affected areas. The private sector can, however, at times have a negative impact, such as the role of foreign businesses in the diamond industries of Angola and Sierra Leone.[4]

295. Protection is a multi-dimensional process involving a range of entities and methods. Central activities include the delivery of humanitarian aid; monitoring, recording and reporting of violations of human rights and international humanitarian law; institution-building, including governance and development programmes; and, potentially, deployment of peacekeeping or peace enforcement troops. The Secretary-General recently identified a series of measures to enhance protection of civilians, including prosecution of

violations of international criminal law; promotion of access to vulnerable populations; separation of civilians and armed elements; and responsible use of media and information in conflict situations.[5] A series of Security Council resolutions further demonstrates a growing awareness by the United Nations of the range and complexity of protection issues.[6]

296. Women's protection needs, and their risk and experiences of violence differ in significant ways from those of men, as outlined in Chapter II. The gender perspectives in each of the activities undertaken in the framework of protection therefore need to be explicitly identified and addressed. For example, protection from, and prevention of, violence including gender-based and sexual violence, necessitates monitoring and reporting all forms of violence against women and girls, and setting up mechanisms for addressing needs created by violence, including counselling, legal, medical and other forms of material support.

Relief distribution and access to resources and benefits

297. Effective distribution of relief, and of other benefits, requires an understanding of the gender dimensions of specific crises in order to identify and assess gender-specific relief needs. Attention should be given to actively involving women in the needs assessment and targeting processes. Special assessment techniques can be used to identify needs among different populations to ensure their participation in planning and relief allocation. Registration of refugees and displaced people, when made in the name of a male head of household, can result in exclusion of women from control over the distribution of basic goods and services, literacy programmes, economic and employment opportunities, and project management and administration. As communities are being rebuilt, women's equal access to water and shelter are also critical.

298. Women and girls often have different experiences than men and boys during displacement and flight. They may have unequal access to relief aid and food security and be forced to engage in prostitution for essential goods and services. There can be risks involved in the performance of daily tasks in camps where their protection and survival needs have not been taken into account in the overall design of camps and distribution sites. Failure to identify and address the specific needs and priorities of women and men can have serious negative effects on the health and well-being of women and girls.

299. Humanitarian programmes, particularly if designed on the basis of data inadequately disaggregated by sex and age, as well as gaps in relevant information on women and girls, can reinforce or exacerbate existing gender-based discrimination. One example of such inadvertent discrimination is related to civil status. Where assistance is distributed to families only, some women and girls have no choice but to marry men they do not know, trust or care for, and unaccompanied girls are obliged to join households in camps and settlements. In other situations, women have become pregnant in order to qualify for supplemental food rations, with the response of the agency concerned being an emphasis on family planning, rather than a focus on the cause – inadequate food supply or inappropriate systems of distribution. In past situations, where the military or armed leadership controlled food distribution, disparities resulted between the health and nutritional status of the combatants and other armed groups on the one hand, and those of uprooted women and children on the other.

300. In some parts of the world, humanitarian agencies have encountered resistance from both government authorities and rebel factions in their efforts to provide medical assistance, education or work opportunities to women or girls. The challenge for the international community is to respond in a consistent and coordinated manner, based on the principles of non-discrimination and equality between women and men.

Livelihoods, food security and health

301. Humanitarian operations must be aware of, and respond adequately, to the gender issues that arise in relation to livelihoods, food security and health in conflict and post-conflict situations. The linkage between livelihoods, food security and health should also be identified and addressed.

302. Armed conflict has a negative impact on livelihoods. Employment in formal economies shrinks, and competition in informal economies heightens. Opportunities need to be provided in refugee camps and other emergency settlements for equitable access to education, training and income generation opportunities. The existing skills of women refugees and displaced persons, as teachers, nurses, social workers, and others, can be drawn on to create training and skills enhancement opportunities. It is important to ensure that women have opportunities for involvement in development and reconstruction projects, including through access to credit and that their needs and priorities are taken into account in the development and implementation of these projects.[7]

303. Parents also realize that the establishment of schools, however rudimentary they may be, brings routine back into their children's lives. Women stress their need for literacy, skills training and other forms of education, particularly, to engage in informal sector activities. Education is often highlighted as a high priority of displaced families to secure sustainable livelihoods.

304. Household food security is often threatened or diminished by armed conflict, which reduces opportunities for agricultural production and contributes to the breakdown of markets. Support to household food and nutrition security entails the provision of, and access to appropriate and adequate food supplies, including foods that are rich in micronutrients. This can be best accomplished through an analysis of the household food economy to understand specific needs and the role of gender relations within families and households.

305. Armed conflict can greatly affect the physical, reproductive, sexual and mental health of women and girls. Key aspects of sexual and reproductive health that must be taken into account in humanitarian operations to reduce and prevent mortality and morbidity, especially among women and adolescent girls, include safe motherhood, gender-based and sexual violence, STIs, including HIV/AIDS, family planning, managing of complications relating to spontaneous or unsafe abortion, caring for those who have undergone female genital mutilation, and the reproductive health concerns of youth. Health services are needed to protect and enhance well-being of both rural and urban populations affected and displaced by crises.

B. Responses and challenges

306. To be effective, humanitarian responses must focus on a wide range of issues and seek the active involvement of the uprooted and host communities in planning, implementation, monitoring and evaluation of programmes so as to enhance their effectiveness. Adequate humanitarian responses require collaboration between community services workers, protection/human rights officers, and security personnel in support of the participation of uprooted persons in the reconstruction of their countries, including as supporters of enduring peace. Many agencies have put in place tools, such as policies and guidelines, codes of conduct, and training to ensure that gender perspectives and the needs of women are consistently addressed by all staff involved in humanitarian operations. However, many continue to face challenges in the effective utilization of these tools.

307. All too often humanitarian assistance programmes view women as one more category in a list of vulnerable groups, for example: the poor, the homeless, the elderly, children and women. This formulation is problematic on two grounds. First, there are gender dimensions and differences within each of these vulnerable groups that must be understood. The "poor" are made up of both women and men and there are important differences and inequalities between women and men in relation to the causes and effects of poverty and potential copying strategies. Children are made up of both girls and boys and there are important differences and inequalities that need to be identified and addressed. The situations of elderly women and men can be significantly different. Although they may share needs and priorities, women and men, and girls and boys will also have different responsibilities, experiences and needs and different resources they can draw on. Furthermore, there are often important differences among women within each category, based on ethnic group, class, age, religion or position in the conflict that should not be over-looked.

308. Second, the focus on women as a vulnerable group tends to obscure women's capabilities. Throughout the world, women in situations of armed conflict do survive, often shouldering immense responsibilities. One forum noted that "people who live in a war zone often define their daily life as 'resisting war itself.'" [8] Women organize schools, rebuild health centres, and establish solidarity groups to provide food and medicine. Responses to humanitarian crises should recognize and build on existing women's organizations and resources.

United Nations initiatives by entities

309. Acknowledging the fact that women and girls make up the majority of refugee and internally displaced populations, humanitarian and development agencies involved in conflict and post-conflict situations are increasingly reworking existing programmes to better identify and address the protection and assistance needs and rights of women and girls.

310. The Consolidated Appeals Process (CAP) is a coordination tool established to set common objectives and strategies for humanitarian assistance, and for joint resource mobilization for the United Nations system in partnership with other humanitarian actors in a country or region. Over the ten years of its existence, more than 165 appeals have been issued. The 2001 CAP theme "Women and War" was chosen in recognition of the special needs and important contributions of women in emergency situations. Dur-

ing 2001 and 2002, the Reference Group on Gender and Humanitarian Assistance of the IASC focused on mainstreaming gender perspectives in CAP and, as a result, revised the Capacities and Vulnerabilities Analysis (CVA) tool for use in the CAP workshops.

311. The primary challenge for humanitarian agencies is to accord explicit attention to gender perspectives in all policies and guidelines applicable to humanitarian situations. This is particularly important for the CAP documents as they set common objectives and strategies for humanitarian assistance in a country.

312. Over the last decade, several key United Nations agencies and some Member States' agencies and NGOs have made it a priority to include refugee and displaced women among those planning and carrying out policies and programmes. Most notable among these are UNHCR's series of consultations with refugee, displaced and returnee women,[9] and the World Food Programme's (WFP's) goal that 80 per cent of all relief food should be provided directly to women and the placement of women in leading roles in distribution of foodstuffs. Government development programmes are also increasingly paying attention to the role of women in food security.

313. From its experience in adopting a community-based approach to identifying, targeting and distributing food aid to beneficiaries that required women to be 50 per cent of the membership in new village relief committees, WFP has concluded that it is crucial to work on several levels of women's participation in targeting and distribution: (a) increased representation in decision-making forums; (b) active participation in decision-making by expressing their opinions; and (c) being effectively heard and actually influencing decisions.

314. The UNIFEM African Women in Crisis Umbrella Programme aims at providing women with technical and economic empowerment skills, including skills development in non-traditional economic activities, such as carpentry and construction. It also includes training in project management, resource mobilization, and advocacy to help facilitate the emergence of women's networks and mutual support systems.

315. IOM has instituted the Widows Assistance Programme in Cambodia to help address the needs of an estimated 7,000 to 9,000 dependent families of deceased soldiers on the basis of a gender analysis of the situation of these widows, and has made recommendations regarding vocational training, adult literacy training, and micro-credit loans to facilitate their economic empowerment.

316. Despite some progress in gender mainstreaming in humanitarian operations, in many agencies the focus is still on specific projects for women and girls, rather than the full acknowledgement of the needs and priorities in existing programmes. Accurate assessment is a basic component of all humanitarian assistance planning and implementation. It requires that all agencies ensure that from initial appraisal and planning phases, compilation of data across all sectors is broken down by sex, age, and other appropriate categories, in order to understand and address the specific and differential impact of the particular crisis situation on the various groups in the community. In programme planning and budgeting and reporting, it is critical to explicitly identify gender perspectives, outline the means by which these will be addressed and clearly indicate resource allocations. In monitoring and evaluation, it is also important to consider the differential impact of intervention strategies on women and men and to indicate the amount of expenditure, as well as the type of relief commodities that have been distributed to, and utilized by, different sections of the community.[10]

Policies, operational strategies and guidelines

317. In many humanitarian agencies specific policies, strategies and guidelines have been developed on incorporating gender perspectives in humanitarian situations. A further constraint is that, in some instances, United Nations organizations subcontract to non-governmental operating partners that do not have, or fail to enforce, similar standards and guidelines.

318. In 1999, the Inter-Agency Standing Committee Policy Statement on mainstreaming gender perspectives into humanitarian response committed its member agencies to produce gender-sensitive operational studies, good practice examples, guidelines and checklists for programming, as well as the establishment of instruments and mechanisms for monitoring and evaluation, such as gender-impact methodologies. It also called for the incorporation of gender analysis techniques in other institutional tools and procedures.

319. The Inter-Agency Standing Committee Reference Group on Gender and Humanitarian Assistance,[11] established in 1998, provides support to the integration of gender perspectives into humanitarian assistance and disseminates key materials on gender mainstreaming. In order to ensure linkages with other relevant IASC subsidiary bodies, one Reference Group member, the United Nations Children's Fund (UNICEF) is a member of the IASC Task Force on Protection from Sexual Exploitation and Abuse in

Humanitarian Crises. WFP developed, on behalf of the Reference Group, an electronic Gender and Humanitarian Assistance Resource Kit, which is posted on Reliefweb[12] for access to humanitarian workers in the field.

320. UNFPA, UNHCR, UNICEF and the World Health Organization (WHO) have developed guidelines and documented best practices relating to health care issues for women and girls in emergency situations. UNFPA's materials for emergency relief responses were developed under the framework of reproductive health and family planning as basic human rights. In 2001, UNFPA held a consultative group meeting on the impact of armed conflict on women and girls and mainstreaming gender perspectives in reproductive health and population programmes in areas of conflict and rehabilitation.

321. A special inter-agency Working Group on Reproductive Health in Refugee Situations has been established. Its members – over 30 United Nations agencies and NGOs – have collaborated to produce an inter-agency field manual on reproductive health in refugee situations[13] in which reproductive health care for women, girls, men and boys is framed as a human rights issue. The manual provides detailed information and practices on such issues as safe motherhood, gender-based and sexual violence, STIs, including HIV/AIDS, family planning, and the reproductive health concerns of young people. [14]

322. The Food and Agriculture Organization (FAO), UNHCR, UNICEF and WFP have prepared gender-sensitive guidelines regarding nutrition and food security.

323. A variety of agencies have developed policies and guidelines regarding protection, monitoring and reporting on violence against women and girls. UNHCR developed guidelines on the protection of refugee women in 1991, and on prevention and response to sexual violence against refugees in 1995. It also conducted a series of dialogues with refugee women to learn more about their concerns and priorities on these matters. The Guiding Principles on Internal Displacement, formulated by the Special Representative on internally displaced persons, also address the various needs of internally displaced women.

324. UNICEF formulated guidelines on the protection of children and internally displaced women, has developed training materials for peacekeepers, and is preparing materials regarding gender-aware disarmament, demobilization, and reintegration strategies for former boy and girl soldiers. WFP

has developed Commitments to Women, including women in emergency situations.

325. NGOs, such as CARE, OXFAM, Save the Children/UK, and others, have also developed gender-sensitive tools for use in humanitarian situations. Guidelines for a field manual for monitoring and reporting on violations of the rights of women during armed conflict have been developed by Amnesty International and the International Centre for Human Rights and Democratic Development, and Human Rights Watch has created a manual on monitoring and reporting violations. The Women's Commission for Refugee Women and Children has produced guidelines on the gender-sensitive set-up of camps for refugees and internally displaced persons.

326. Where United Nations departments and agencies involved in humanitarian operations do have policies and guidelines on women and girls, their implementation is fragmented and inconsistent to systematically follow-up on implementation of existing guidelines, including through development of reporting and accountability mechanisms. A number of studies have found that greater awareness on the existence of such policies, strategies and guidelines needs to be promoted and priority given to promoting and ensuring their widespread use. [15]

327. For example, UNHCR's guidelines on the protection of refugee women should be a standard part of that agency's refugee work. An assessment of ten years of implementation of the UNHCR Policy on Refugee Women and Guidelines on their Protection published in May 2002 documented positive examples of enhanced protection activities in accordance with the Guidelines, but also a number of negative examples. Overall, implementation was found to be uneven and incomplete, occurring on an ad hoc basis in certain sites rather than in a globally consistent and systematic way. [16]

328. Studies undertaken by United Nations agencies also identify the lack of clearly defined and measurable objectives on the basis of global policy statements as a primary reason for failure to implement gender mainstreaming strategies. Development of more clearly defined goals and accountability measures must therefore be a top priority. Renewed commitment from senior officials to achieving these goals is also important. [17]

Standards of conduct

329. Like civilian staff in peacekeeping operations, civilian staff in humanitarian operations are bound by the Code of Conduct for International Civil Servants, in addition to United Nations rules and regulations which refer to the "highest standards of integrity and conduct" expected of United Nations staff. Currently, the standards, codes of conduct and mechanisms for how to respond to actions of staff vary greatly among different agencies involved in humanitarian operations. Additionally, the United Nations is only a part of the overall humanitarian response which is carried out by numerous humanitarian agencies, thus making collective responsibility for staff conduct exceedingly difficult.

330. Recent events have demonstrated that more specific and more strictly enforced codes of conduct are needed. In response to recent allegations of abuse of women and children by humanitarian workers in the Mano River region, an Inter-Agency Standing Committee Task Force on Protection from Sexual Exploitation and Abuse in Humanitarian Crises was established in March 2002 with a goal of developing a Plan of Action. The Inter-Agency Standing Committee recognized that the problem of sexual exploitation and abuse in humanitarian crises is not confined to West Africa but is a global problem. Sexual exploitation and abuse are embedded in unequal power relationships. The lack of economic opportunities for displaced populations and the loss of social protection further exacerbate the potential for abuse. Responses are thus required from many different actors to achieve "a shift in the organizational culture and approach of humanitarian agencies".[18]

331. The Plan of Action, which has been endorsed by all humanitarian agencies, contains six principles which all members of the Inter-Agency Standing Committee are required to incorporate into codes of conduct:

1. Sexual exploitation and abuse by humanitarian workers constitute acts of gross misconduct and are therefore grounds for termination of employment.

2. Sexual activity with children (persons under the age of 18) is prohibited regardless of the age of majority or age of consent locally. Mistaken belief in the age of a child is not a defence.

3. Exchange of money, employment, goods, or services for sex, including sexual favours or other forms of humiliating, degrading

or exploitative behavior is prohibited. This includes exchange of assistance that is due to beneficiaries.

4.   Sexual relationships between humanitarian workers and beneficiaries are strongly discouraged since they are based on inherently unequal power dynamics. Such relationships undermine the credibility and integrity of humanitarian aid work.

5.   Where a humanitarian worker develops concerns or suspicions regarding sexual abuse or exploitation by a fellow worker, whether in the same agency or not, s/he must report such concerns via established agency reporting mechanisms.

6.   Humanitarian workers are obliged to create and maintain an environment which prevents sexual exploitation and abuse and promotes the implementation of their code of conduct. Managers at all levels have particular responsibilities to support and develop systems which maintain this environment.

332. Based on the Plan of Action, the Inter-Agency Standing Committee will expect its humanitarian agency members to integrate principles and standards of behaviour into codes of conduct and staff rules and to ensure that these principles are disseminated and integrated into personnel and administrative standards as well as in agreements with partners and contractors. The Plan of Action could also become a guide to monitor and evaluate the implementation of new or revised codes of conduct. In addition, the Plan of Action could serve as a basis for discussions beyond the humanitarian community with host governments, donors and peacekeepers on measures to address the problem of sexual exploitation and abuse.

333. UNICEF is developing training for country programme offices that explains the context and factors that contribute to sexual abuse and exploitation in humanitarian crises, provides opportunities to discuss the core principles and explores programming strategies to minimize the potential for abuse and exploitation.

334. One of the main challenges remains the question of accountability towards beneficiaries and host governments at individual agency level and through inter-agency coordination. Currently, there are few avenues of recourse for beneficiaries in cases of exploitation by humanitarian workers. Mechanisms for reporting complaints, investigative procedures and disciplinary processes are also required.

Recruitment and training

335. Although reports from United Nations humanitarian and development agencies find that female participation in key positions, such as protection officers, health staff, food distribution officers, specialist staff, advisers and interpreters is critical, women's representation in field offices and on the ground in humanitarian operations is poor. The presence of women staff in positions of authority, being respectfully and equitably treated by their male counterparts, can underline the importance of equality and non-discrimination. This is especially important in situations where the responsibilities, roles and rights of women and adolescent girls have expanded due to the conflict, as was the case in Rwanda and most recently in Afghanistan.

336. The appointment of gender specialists in field locations helps to ensure that the rights of women and girls are upheld, that abuses of their rights are monitored and reported, and that relevant gender perspectives are identified and addressed in all humanitarian activities.[19]

337. Evidence suggests that while many United Nations personnel are sympathetic to the needs of women and girls in their workplace, they do not have a clear understanding of the impacts of conflict and post-conflict situations on women and girls or its specific experiences of women and girls during humanitarian operations. Consequently, they do not know how to address gender issues in their day-to-day work. The need for specialized training, including on the gender-sensitive design of camp facilities and on landmine programmes, has been emphasized.

Recommendations

Action 1:   Ensure that agencies of the United Nations and other international organizations, regional organizations and NGOs have safe and unhindered access to populations in need, especially women and girls.

Action 2:   Increase the participation of women and girls, fully utilize their capacities, and give attention to their needs and priorities, from the initial stages of programming and service delivery and advocacy activities in humanitarian crises, in order to optimise the benefits for women and girls.

Action 3:   Increase the focus on and resources for the protection of women and girls from gender-based and sexual violence, including through attention to the risks faced by women and girls, in particular related to sexual violence, abuse and exploitation, in initial needs assessments, and through the development of strategies to minimize these risks and reduce the vulnerability of women and girls, including through the provision of training on culturally appropriate interview techniques and trauma counselling and the use of female personnel (as protection officers, medical personnel, and interpreters).

Action 4: Integrate prevention activities into all areas of emergency response, including in design of camps, provision of shelter, sanitation facilities and health-care facilities, distribution of food supplies and other benefits, access to water supplies, as well as specific protection programmes, working together with health service providers, NGOs and community groups, including women's groups and networks, to address both discrimination against women and girls and the effects of gender-based and sexual violence.

Action 5: Increase the capacities of women and girls affected by armed conflict to protect themselves from the risk of HIV/AIDS, principally through protection from sexual violence, abuse and exploitation, access to treatment and the provision of health care services, including sexual and reproductive health, and through HIV/AIDS prevention education that promotes gender equality within a culture- and gender-sensitive framework.

Action 6: Increase the provision of reproductive health services, which take into account the specific vulnerabilities of women and girls in conflict and post-conflict situations of women and girls.

Action 7: Ensure access to appropriate and adequate health care for victims of rape and other gender-based and sexual violence, including culturally sensitive counselling in a supportive environment which ensures confidentiality, as an integral component of reproductive health services.

Action 8: Restore and strengthen safe access to education for girls and adolescent girls as a priority component of all humanitarian assistance, ensuring that the core curriculum includes gender-sensitive training on life skills, family life education, landmine awareness, HIV/AIDS and other STI prevention, human rights, peace education as well as psychological support.

Action 9: Address the special needs of girls affected by armed conflict in the design of recovery assistance programmes, in particular girls who are heads of households, internally displaced, refugees, unaccompanied, separated, or orphaned, as well as girls who have been sexually exploited and used as combatants, including through the allocation of sufficient resources.

Action 10: Provide opportunities for women and girls as well as men and boys to expand their capabilities and develop skills to better prepare them for returning to their homes and communities.

Action 11: Provide women and girls with identity cards or other essential documents to enable them to register and be eligible for assistance, and address problems of nationality faced by women and their children.

Action 12: Take steps to ensure that elderly women are provided protection and that their specific needs for relief services are met.

Action 13: Take steps to prevent the recruitment of girls and boys into armed forces and rebel groups, in particular orphans, unaccompanied, separated, refugee, displaced and street children, including by ensuring access to education and vocational training.

Action 14: Ensure that assessments leading to Consolidated Appeals Processes incorporate attention to the situation of women and girls in conflict and post-conflict situations.

Action 15: Promote utilization of existing strategies and guidelines on the protection of refugee and displaced women by all humanitarian agencies, including through the provision of training and establishment of monitoring and accountability mechanisms.

Action 16: Promote inter-agency collaboration on development, dissemination and implementation of policies, strategies and utilization of guidelines and other materials, and increase exchange of information and good practice examples.

Action 17: Enforce implementation of the Plan of Action developed by the Inter-Agency Standing Committee Task Force on Protection from Sexual Exploitation and Abuse in Humanitarian Crises, and require regular monitoring and reporting on progress.

Action 18: Provide humanitarian staff and local volunteers with comprehensive and appropriate training on gender perspectives, including the different forms of human rights abuses that women and girls face during and after conflict, particularly gender-based and sexual violence.

Action 19: Ensure that humanitarian organizations responsible for provision of immediate relief systematically include attention to gender-based and sexual violence in all research, data collection and documentation, including through regular consultations with health facilities, midwives, traditional birth attendants, and women's groups and networks.

VII. Reconstruction and Rehabilitation

338. Discrimination against women and girls and gender inequalities can persist or deepen during the period after conflict, thereby limiting the opportunities women and adolescent girls have to play significant roles in the design and implementation of peace and reconstruction processes.[1] Women and girls compared with men and boys have unequal access to resources during and after conflict. Men are usually better placed to be involved in, and benefit from, reconstruction initiatives, often because of their greater participation in public life before conflict. Men also tend to have greater control over economic resources and more education than women. However, there have been situations in which women and girls and their organizations and networks have been able to share in shaping political, economic and social reconstruction processes. Sustainable and durable peace requires the participation of women and girls, as well as the integration of gender perspectives in all reconstruction processes. Reconstruction efforts which are based on human rights principles, including non-discrimination, can avoid perpetuating situations of inequality and discrimination and lead to the creation of more equitable and sustainable societies.

A. Political, civil and judicial reconstruction

339. The period of transition after a conflict provides an opportunity to create a democratic and equal society. The *2002 Human Development Report* suggests that key features of such a society include a system of representation, with well-functioning political parties and special interest associations; an electoral system that guarantees free and fair elections, as well as universal suffrage; a system of checks and balances, based on the separation of powers with independent judicial and legislative branches; a vibrant civil society, able to monitor government and private businesses and provide alternative forms of political participation; a free, independent media; and an effective civilian control over the military and other security forces.[2] Central to any transition process is the need to take account of the differential needs of women and men at all stages of rebuilding of societies and the importance of concrete mechanisms to ensure that all people – women and men – enjoy freedoms and participate equally in rehabilitation and reconstruction.[3]

340. Constitutional reform processes during reconstruction should include the participation of women and take account of gender perspectives. In addition to establishing the legal framework of the State, Constitutions frequently include bills of rights which define political, civil, economic, social, cultural and religious rights, and provide mechanisms to enforce those rights. In Cambodia, a consultative process, including women of all socio-economic classes and from all parts of the country, accompanied the drafting of the Constitution during the UNTAC operational period. As a result, the current Cambodian Constitution grants women equal rights with men. Similarly, in Eritrea and South Africa, the formulation of the Constitutions prompted a high level of public discussion involving women, men and, to a lesser extent, older adolescent girls and boys from all regions, including those in the diaspora. The Eritrean Constitution recognizes the equal rights of women and men, and also grants women the right of access to land, prohibits female circumcision, dowry and bride price, and provides for maternity leave.[4]

341. Other legislation should also be prepared from a gender perspective and its preparation should involve the participation of women. Existing laws which discriminate against women and girls should be repealed or amended. Legislation to address specific areas, such as violence against women, particularly domestic and sexual violence, harmful traditional practices, marriage, divorce, custody, property and inheritance rights, should be formulated. Nationality laws should ensure that women retain their right to independent nationality on marriage, and grant them equal rights with men with respect to the nationality of their children. Nationality laws should also be flexible in order to provide for family reunion. Legislative change must be accompanied by legal literacy programmes for women and girls and the establishment of institutions that provide legal education and counselling to women, girls and civil society organizations.

342. A gender-sensitive judiciary is critical to remove gender bias within courts which curbs the rights of women and girls and perpetuates discrimination and inequality. In some post-conflict contexts, women and adolescent girls have not received favourable court decisions regarding custody of children, rights to property or inheritance, or the right to be free of violence. In Kosovo, for example, husbands or fathers accused of sexual or physical violence were not convicted in criminal trials on grounds of "lack of evidence", despite the presentation of photographs and statements of witnesses.[5] It is important that the appropriate government agencies and judicial structures investigate cases of violations, including violence against

women and girls. Women mobilize around changes to the legal system in post-conflict situations, including reform of the civil and criminal codes to ensure equality before the law, classification of sexual harassment as a criminal offence and the criminalization of sexual and physical abuse by a spouse, partner, parent or guardian. In order to ensure that States respect, and their judiciaries enforce, the various international and domestic legal instruments available to them, judges and legal personnel should be sensitized to raise their awareness of and capacity to address gender issues. This would include efforts to prevent discriminatory treatment by the courts of survivors of violations, including sexual violence during armed conflict, and to ensure that interviews, investigations and court proceedings are carried out in a gender-sensitive manner.[6]

343.   An integral part of reconstruction is the issue of justice for the victims of violations of international humanitarian and human rights law. Impunity for crimes committed against women and girls may occur, at least in part, because of a disregard for the rights of women and girls. Violations of international humanitarian law and human rights should be documented, investigated and prosecuted during reconstruction as this demonstrates to women as well as men, that there is social justice and that mechanisms exist for dealing with the violations they endured during the conflict, including recording them even after the conflict ends.

344.   At the national level, truth and reconciliation commissions have been established as part of some post-conflict reconciliation efforts. They create opportunities for the public recording and acknowledgement of violations and people's suffering. However, this process may not satisfy everyone. Some truth commissions have provided for full amnesty for perpetrators who agree to participate in them. For many observers, as long as the perpetrators of violence and sexual violence are allowed to act with impunity, for example, in the cases of Guatemala, Sierra Leone and Uganda, victims of that violence, including women and girls, will have been denied justice. Other communities have found amnesties of value because they allow them to move forward from the conflicts, for example, in Uganda where amnesty laws for the Lord's Resistance Army were enacted.

345.   Equitable access to truth commissions or other legal proceedings may be particularly problematic for women and adolescent girls who wish to testify but fear reprisals from their unpunished torturers and rapists who often continue living alongside them.[7] There are also difficulties, such as heightened feelings of fear or shame, faced by women and adolescent girls who come forward and testify about the violations that occurred. Employing

gender-sensitive procedures can mitigate these difficulties. Women and girls should be questioned individually, and by persons trained to work with abused women and girls. Ways of enabling women to speak about their experiences without revisiting the full horror of their torture, terror, humiliation or abuse should be sought. Group hearings can, for example, make it easier for women and girls to come forward. Whatever the means used, women and girls should be clearly advised of the measures put in place to ensure confidentiality of the processes of their testimony.[8]

346. Post-conflict reconstruction also involves the creation or reconstruction of civil society, which usually involves the support and enhancement of local NGOs. However, a major challenge in supporting the development of civil society in many countries is the lack of proper legislation regarding NGOs which constrains recognition of the organizations by international and private donors. Many newly established NGOs have poor levels of internal organization, are under-resourced and highly dependent on international funding, and require technical assistance to strengthen their capacities. Communication between Governments and NGOs can be difficult if there is mistrust on both sides. Limited funds can also generate strong antagonism between different NGOs that find themselves competing for those scarce resources.[9] Newly formed women's groups and networks face these constraints, as well as the constraints and obstacles that are particular to organizing as women, including scepticism about the concerns of women and girls and their ability to organize around them. International actors involved in supporting local NGOs need to identify and support organizing efforts of women.[10]

347. A central part of post-conflict reconstruction is the creation of an electoral system which guarantees free and fair elections, and allows for universal suffrage. Women have the right to vote, but may not be granted full rights to political participation, or face resistance if they seek public office. Officials in Somalia strongly opposed women representing their clan in the Transitional Council, although in previous governments the country had female ministers. In Cambodia, only 5 per cent of the candidates for the elections to the Assembly were women, and the Supreme National Council had no women members.[11] More positively, in East Timor, through the combined efforts of the women's civil society organizations, the UNTAET mission and United Nations entities, women account for 27 per cent of the new Constituent Assembly. One measure to increase women's political participation is the introduction of quota for women candidates in local and national elections. Such quota can be voluntary targets established by political

parties or legislated percentages in local councils and parliaments. Affirmative action was applied successfully by UNMIK to increase women's representation in the Kosovo Assembly. However, in order to be sustainable, such measures need to be coupled with training for women candidates and women in public office; public awareness raising campaigns; and changes within political parties.

348. Post-conflict reconstruction often includes the reorganization of military and police institutions. Military forces should be representative of the nation's population and must include strong adherence to international humanitarian law and human rights standards, including the rights of women and girls, with clear enforcement mechanisms. Efforts with respect to police structures should focus on creating accountable and representative police forces and replacing repressive, existing security forces. This is particularly important for women and girls because security forces have often been involved in international humanitarian law and human rights violations against women and girls, including sexual violence, torture and mutilations.

349. The equitable representation of women on most of these security and police forces has not improved. In Haiti, only 7 per cent of the new police force are women, a majority of whom serve as desk officers or traffic police. In El Salvador, the number of women in the police force has fallen from 7 per cent to under 6 per cent. Increasing the representation of women within security forces is important for a variety of reasons, including in order to be able to deal adequately with the high levels of domestic battering and sexual assaults that increase in post-conflict situations. Demobilized, unemployed guerilias or government soldiers often abuse their partners to express their economic and social frustration. In these situations, violence may be more readily reported to women police officers than to male officers.[12]

B. Economic reconstruction

350. Armed conflict usually results in significant damage to overall economic infrastructure. Physical damage alone has a profound economic impact. Reconstruction efforts often include macro-economic support, strengthening of economic institutions and infrastructure reconstruction along with micro-level initiatives to try to generate employment, build marketable skills, and support small business development.

351. Efforts to understand the gender dimensions of post-conflict economic reconstruction require a clear understanding of the pre-conflict economy

and how it changed during the war. Crucial dimensions include the general position of women and men in the economy (across and within sectors, urban and rural patterns, formal and informal economies), differential vocational skills and educational profiles, access to capital, social attitudes to men and women's work, the distribution of domestic responsibilities and how this affects women's and men's work lives, and different mobility patterns for women and men. Given these differences and inequalities in markets and economic institutions, as well as economic policies that can easily neglect gender perspectives, men and women are often affected differently by economic reform and by international support to rebuild economies.

352. Just as in all other sectors, it is important to understand the concrete nature of issues in economic reconstruction. The situation of the economy, and of women and men within the economy, differs from country to country. A context-specific approach is important.

353. In post-conflict contexts, economic pressures, including resumption of debt servicing, affect the funding available for social services and for the broader structure of economies, for example, when export production is given priority over subsistence or domestic consumption production. Structural adjustment policies and assistance, which is conditioned on reform of governments and economies, may negatively impact on the immediate and long-term economic and social well-being of women and girls.[13]

354. The shrinking of the public sector tends to have a negative impact on employment opportunities in urban and rural areas. Reduction and dismantling of State-financed social services increases pressure on the private sector to undertake those functions, which often results in higher prices, in worsened quality or unavailability of services. This places greater demands on women to make up for lost services in their homes.[14]

355. International reconstruction initiatives often provide new labour opportunities for women or adolescent girls, for example, as translators, secretaries, and mid-level programme administrators. On the other hand, large-scale intervention, particularly the influx of foreign aid workers, troops and currency can significantly distort and undermine local economies where women are particularly active.[15] For example, in East Timor, women and adolescent girls dominate the informal sector as housekeepers, cooks, childcare providers, and restaurant and hotel staff servicing internationals associated with the peacekeeping operation. With the downsizing and eventual liquidation of the mission, there will be considerable economic impact on

women, girls and their families as many of them are the sole income provider for their families.[16]

356. The formal economy is usually the sector that is the hardest hit during conflict as capital flight leads to high unemployment. During conflict, women's employment opportunities in the formal sector can increase if institutions employ women and adolescent girls to replace men and adolescent boys who have been lost in the conflict or have entered the fighting forces. In the post-conflict period, maintaining positions or finding work in the formal economy can be difficult for women and girls. In countries like Bosnia and Herzegovina and Mozambique, the combination of these factors resulted in steep reversal of positive employment trends for women in the formal economy in the post-conflict phase.[17]

357. Even when women and adolescent girls are part of the formal economy, there may be marked differences in attitudes towards their employment after conflict. After the formal conclusion of peace accords, women and adolescent girls who fought and worked side by side with men and adolescent boys may be expected to stay at home and fulfil family responsibilities. Advances in employment opportunities of the economy do not keep pace with the demand for jobs from male ex-combatants. Women and adolescent girls who, for different reasons, do not retreat into their homes may be considered problems.[18]

358. Efforts by external actors may be the only way to minimize discrimination against particular segments of the labour market, for example, by building roads to facilitate marketing of products from remote rural areas or extending credit and training to female entrepreneurs. In agricultural societies, small-scale farmers, many of whom are women, need support to ensure food security.

359. In the aftermath of conflict, effects of the mining of agricultural fields, extensive environmental damage, the destruction of farm equipment and the theft of animals contribute to the constraints faced by small-scale farmers, including women. With the loss of male family members, women or girl-headed households may encounter legal and cultural barriers to retaining and cultivating their lands and obtaining farming implements or agricultural inputs. At times they may be dispossessed of their lands and have to shift to casual agricultural labour, which erodes their material and social positions.[19]

360. During reconstruction, women and girls participate extensively in informal sector activities, such as petty trading, small-scale food production,

and provision of services. These activities do not require large capital investments and the time period between investment and economic gain is relatively short. Many rural people, including women and their families, migrate to urban centres in order to gain greater access to informal markets. In these urban settings women and adolescent girls may not have adequate social networks to draw upon for assistance and may have difficulties in benefiting fully from the new opportunities.

361. When the rates of employment of women are growing and those of men are declining in both the formal and informal sectors, and when there are large numbers of unemployed male ex-combatants, women's economic activities may lead to increased tensions between women and men.[20] This is especially so if women are active in areas previously dominated by men.

362. During post-conflict periods many women and adolescent girls are in need of skills training for income-generating activities. Special programmes for credit and income-generating skills that target women and adolescent girls have been prone to design flaws, such as the lack of market feasibility, and have led to resistance from men who have prevented their wives or daughters from participating in training courses.[21] In El Salvador and Eritrea, lack of childcare in contexts where women were solely responsible for parenting made it almost impossible for women to participate in training or work outside the home.[22]

363. Existing legal and social barriers for women and adolescent girls to employment and educational opportunities do not vanish with the end of the conflict. Targeted legislation and other interventions are needed to overcome these barriers. Legislation is necessary to enable women and adolescent girls to receive credit, to buy, rent or inherit land and property, and to be legally recognized as heads of households, widows, divorcees and parents or guardians.[23] Afghanistan, during the regime of the Taliban, is an extreme example of the denial of the right to work and basic social services that women and girls were forced to endure both during conflict and upon entry into the post-conflict period.

C. Social reconstruction

364. Social reconstruction includes the reconstruction of damaged or destroyed social sectors, including health care, education and social service institutions, and involves a long-term process of social healing and reintegration. The severe disruption to social networks caused by armed conflict contributes in the post-conflict period to growing numbers of marginal-

ized groups, including war widows, child-headed households, orphans, the disabled and child soldiers.

Reconstruction of the social sector

365. Health care facilities and workers may be targeted during conflict and thus there is often reduced primary health care available in post-conflict situations.[24] The establishment or re-establishment of a functioning health care system is an important priority in post-conflict situations because of serious health care needs (some ongoing and some caused directly by the conflict).

366. There are psycho-social health problems, disabilities and health issues caused by the culmulative effect of neglecting health issues during the conflict. Physical and psychological health effects of war are carried into the post-conflict periods. Studies from conflict areas have found that women and girls suffer more than men and boys from reproductive and sexual health problems due to poor nutrition, sanitation and sexual abuse, and that men and boys experience problems due to injuries received during the fighting, including shrapnel, bullet and machete wounds.[25]

367. Where health care facilities are damaged or non-existent, women usually take responsibility for continuing to provide basic care to their families and neighbours, using their extended social networks.[26] Women and adolescent girls have mobilized to address the health problems arising from, or increasing with conflict, including the effects of gender-based violence and psychosocial trauma due to violence and displacement.

368. Numerous lessons have been learned on how to ensure that health assistance is sensitive to and meets the needs of all people. Issues, such as appropriate access, investments, proper training, sufficient numbers of women health care workers and adequate supplies have been raised. A challenge is to apply these general lessons to post-conflict health reconstruction.

369. There has been significant international interest in providing health services to women who have survived sexual violence. Experience has shown, however, that in order to be effective this support must be designed with local expertise and be grounded in local realities, experiences and cultures. Models imported from other regions are not immediately applicable.[27]

370. Education is a critical resource for stabilizing communities, rebuilding economies and building peace. Women stress that education for themselves and their children is a top priority during reconstruction. Both girls and boys show great desire to return to school.[28] Just as there is a vast body of lessons on the gender dimensions of the health sector, there are also analyses and guides on how and why gender issues are relevant in education initiatives. These insights, which require adaptation to the post-conflict period, can be useful. Particular areas of concern include education policy/ investments curricula, access of both boys and girls to schools, and teacher training. For example, teacher training and education programmes need to take into account the differences in the experiences of women and girls and men and boys during the conflict. Development of teacher sensitization programmes and appropriate classroom materials that promote understanding of gender equality in the context of community-building can help address some of the inequalities and biases that may have been exacerbated during the conflict.

371. In some cases, girls may be denied their right to education because of social, cultural, religious or political restrictions. In situations of poverty it has proven difficult for families to support the enrolment of girls in schools over sustained periods because of the need for their labour inputs. In the absence of economic growth that increases the proportion of household income provided by able-bodied adults, families cannot afford to lose the contribution to household food and economic security that girls provide. Lack of money for books, clothes or fees, in addition to the need for the labour of adolescents and younger girls in the household, leads to high drop-out rates in post-conflict situations.[29]

372. Women have organized to address these issues. In Sierra Leone, for instance, women mobilized their own resources to rebuild schools that had been destroyed during the war to help ensure their children's education, particularly that of girls. In Rwanda, women survivors of the genocide formed associations to help reconstruct their societies, including literacy and education projects, rebuilding of homes, and programmes for income-generation and psychosocial support.[30]

Social healing and reintegration

373. Support to the reconstruction process necessitates greater understanding of the ways in which communities, households and individuals have been affected by conflict. Changes in power relations take place within communities and households, which create opportunities, but also new roles

in some contexts for women in the post-conflict period. In many cases, household composition has changed due, for example, to remarriages during the conflict. Children and dependants may have been added to the family while others may have been abandoned.[31] Rural to urban migration may increase, with urban dynamics often markedly different from those in rural areas. Because of the lack of rights to land and property and employment opportunities young people, and young women in particular, may be more susceptible to exploitation or abuse, such as trafficking, prostitution or other illicit activities.

374. Refugees and the internally displaced may also seek to return to their former homes and lands. Many return to find their home environments hostile to them, with others having occupied their homes and lands. The climate of suspicion makes it increasingly difficult for returnees to rebuild their homes and lives. At times, it is believed that those who left were granted special privileges or are returning with wealth, which may lead, as in post-conflict Chad, to women returnees being charged higher prices in the markets.[32]

375. Women and girls experience displacement and return differently from men and boys. Behaviours and skills that women and adolescent girls developed while displaced may be viewed as threatening and result in public criticism, as in post-conflict Guatemala. Men may abandon wives and children upon return, claiming the unions had no legal basis, as occurred in post-conflict Cambodia. Internally displaced and refugee women may find that they have no rights to recover their property, including their homes, and may be forced to surrender custody of their children. Problems may be exacerbated for child-headed households, with girl-headed households particularly marginalized. In such instances, intervention to promote change in national and customary laws that discriminate against women and girls is necessary.

376. The decision to return, integrate or resettle requires consultation with all members of a family. Returning refugees or persons against their will may result in future protection problems.

377. Men often return to the family's country or place of origin in advance to prepare for the family's return, leaving their women and children to fend for themselves. In this situation women and girls may be subjected to abuse, including sexual violence. Refugee women left without support are frequently forced to turn to other means to survive, including begging and prostitution, as some Afghans in Pakistan were forced to do.[33] Mechanisms

are necessary to ensure that women and girls do not have trouble accessing food, shelter, health care and medicine for which they are eligible as a result of the departure of the male head of household. Diligent monitoring by community services is required to provide the first indication of such human rights violations within the family and community.

378. Uprooting can sometimes open up new opportunities for women and adolescent girls as they are forced to take on roles that they would never have anticipated fulfilling before flight. As in the case of demobilized female combatants, many uprooted women and girls are pressured back into their old roles upon return. Frameworks, such as UNHCR's People-Oriented Planning, can facilitate a review of the needs, talents and resources of every group of refugees, returnees and displaced persons (including women and men) during the various stages of flight and return, in order to help them maximize their potential.

D. Responses and challenges

379. The United Nations and the development cooperation community, including international NGOs contribute to post-conflict rehabilitation and reconstruction. Increasingly, United Nations programmes combine an emergency and reconstruction focus. The importance of bringing attention to gender perspectives in humanitarian and emergency operations is accentuated by the fact that these activities often continue as development activities after the emergency has ceased. If gender perspectives have not been included in initial policy discussions and planning processes in humanitarian support, they are usually difficult to incorporate at a later stage of reconstruction.

380. The United Nations system's involvement in Afghanistan exemplifies the linkages between humanitarian assistance and development cooperation, and the importance of explicit attention to gender perspectives and the needs of women from the conflict to the reconstruction and development phases. The United Nations inter-agency gender mission to Afghanistan in 1997 aimed to develop a principle-centred approach to the provision of international assistance to Afghanistan in the face of the restrictions imposed on women by the Taliban regime. The United Nations system actively supported women's participation in the peace-building efforts for that country, as discussed in earlier chapters. Many United Nations entities that had provided humanitarian and emergency assistance for women during the Taliban regime remain actively involved in the reconstruction of the country.

381. For example, UNFPA procured medical equipment and carried out essential repairs in three hospitals in Kabul to ensure a reduction of maternal mortality. Upon the request of the Ministry of Women's Affairs, UNFPA is establishing reproductive health counselling and services. UNFPA also provides support for girls' education and women's access to training, and encourages attention to women's rights. Long-term goals for UNICEF in Afghanistan include an improved health care network, especially for pregnant women, and an improved legal code to protect the rights of children and women. Initial responses in support of the reopening of schools in March 2002 included the rehabilitation of 200 schools as well as accelerated classes to allow girls to catch up on their studies. Training new teachers is a key priority of the back-to-school campaign, and a teacher training and orientation workshop in Kabul, in January 2002, provided training for 170 women and 70 men teachers.

382. The International Labour Organization (ILO) has established an InFocus Programme (IFP) on crisis response and reconstruction that capitalizes on the capacities of Afghan women in the reconstruction and development processes. Since women's rights and access to the labour market were severely constrained under the Taliban in Afghanistan, ILO's work requires a focus on the needs of educated women who were forced to leave their jobs as well as on illiterate or poorly educated women who have not had access to employment opportunities. The ILO IFP Crisis Programme has initiated a "SOS Computers" programme which includes a computer centre in the Ministry of Women's Affairs. The centre aims to break gender stereotyping by enabling women to enter into a new range of occupations with better prospects for upward mobility. FAO is finalizing an Action Plan for the Early Rehabilitation of Agriculture in Afghanistan, which includes specific actions targeted towards women. A review of the existing situation of women in agriculture and the rural economy is being carried out. FAO is also in the process of establishing data needs for promoting gender-responsive policy and programme activities, and identifying opportunities and constraints for women as partners in food security promotion. The World Bank's "Afghan Female Teachers In-Service Training" project in Peshawar (Pakistan), trains female teachers in the Afghan University, for the Afghan refugee community.

383. Other examples of activities of United Nations entities in situations of post-conflict reconstruction include UNICEF's support for a Colombian project in schools and communities that promotes peace-building. Since 1999 over 10,000 school-aged children and 200 children in protection insti-

tutes have benefited from this training, and 30 peace-building teams have been set up. UNFPA supports initiatives addressing women's and adolescent girls' reproductive health needs and human rights in situations of post-conflict reconstruction, taking into account both women's capabilities and vulnerabilities. UNFPA also supports access to education and skills development for women and girls. Where unemployment is high and opportunities for employment in the formal sector limited, UNDP has supported income-generating activities for women in the informal sector, including through micro-credit programmes, for example in Cambodia and Tajikistan. In post-conflict Guatemala, UNDP has supported a project aimed at eliminating laws that discriminate against women. The work of the National Women's Forum, established by the Peace Accords to promote the participation and representation of women in decision-making, is also supported by this project.

384. In Tajikistan, an FAO project aims to improve food security by providing poor women's groups with support for income-generating activities. The focus of FAO reconstruction activities in Sierra Leone is to improve household food security in the areas most affected by the civil war. Women's groups are supported with food storage, processing and marketing facilities to improve household food security and income-generation.

385. The World Bank's operational policy, Development Cooperation and Conflict, states that the Bank's objective is to support economic and social recovery and sustainable development "with particular attention to the needs of war-affected groups who are especially vulnerable by reasons of gender, age or disability". The Bank has provided grants to projects that specifically target women. The Post-Conflict Fund, for example, has supported the UNDP "Community Action for the Reintegration and Recovery of Youth and Women" in the Democratic Republic of the Congo, which addresses the particular challenges women face when attempting to reintegrate their communities and secure sustainable livelihoods. In the "Women Reconstructing Southern Africa" Programme, capacity-building activities to promote women's leadership in rural villages are being supported. The "War Widows and Welfare" project in Indonesia, helps poor widows recover their economic capacities in areas of Indonesia and East Timor recently affected by violence.

386. As can be seen from the examples provided, many of the efforts to promote gender equality in rehabilitation and reconstruction are targeted interventions, focusing specifically on women and their needs. These interventions are critical to ensuring that women and girls recover, rebuild their

lives and contribute constructively to reconstruction at community and national levels. Such projects are, however, often seriously under-resourced and marginalized in the reconstruction process. For example, the budget of US$6 million of the Bosnian Women's Initiative (a micro-credit and income-generating project for women), while impressive at first glance, has to be placed in the context of the US$45 million spent by the same donors on small business development projects that did not include enterprises headed by women.[34] Initial analyses, data collection exercises, policy development and programme planning in reconstruction programmes must include attention to the specific problems women and girls face in reintegration and rehabilitation after conflict. These must be addressed both in mainstream interventions and through specific targeted interventions which require adequate resource allocations and other support.

387. Much less is known about the efforts being made by United Nations entities to systematically and explicitly incorporate gender perspectives into the mainstream policy frameworks, strategies and programming processes which guide the choice of activities and resource allocations in reconstruction phases. The extent to which gender perspectives are factored into the design and implementation of programmes on the ground in all areas of reconstruction needs to be more systematically monitored.

388. There are important gender perspectives which should be raised in all the sectors the United Nations entities are engaged in post-conflict contexts – governance, economic and financial sector reform, rural development, agriculture, environment, energy, roads and infrastructure, health, nutrition, education, water and sanitation, and private sector development. In some cases the gender perspectives are relatively well-established and strategies for addressing them are well-developed, particularly in social sectors. In other areas, such as governance and economic reconstruction, more careful thought is required to identify and adequately address all relevant gender perspectives. The well-documented insights on gender mainstreaming in development policies and programmes in non-conflict contexts should be applied in this work.

389. Identifying and addressing gender perspectives in the economic restructuring and reform process is critical to ensure that the needs and priorities of women as well as men are met. Micro-credit should not be seen as a panacea for increasing women's access to economic resources and incorporating gender perspectives in economic development. Women's full representation in economic decision-making requires sustained attention.

390. Gender perspectives should be integrated into all support to budget processes in line with the outcome of the International Conference on Financing for Development held in Monterrey in March 2002.

391. It is particularly important that gender perspectives are fully integrated into initial surveys, appraisals and assessment missions in reconstruction efforts. Pressure to design programmes rapidly should not lead to neglect of gender perspectives. It is at the initial assessment and planning stage that data is collected, basic analysis carried out, policies and strategies developed, activities identified and, most important, resources allocated. If gender perspectives are not taken up at the early planning stage, it is difficult to give adequate attention to them later on in the process. In this context, it is critical that gender perspectives are integrated into the United Nations Development Assistance Framework (UNDAF) process, in the preparation of the Common Country Assessments, the work of thematic groups and the identification of common key indicators.

392. While many multilateral organizations provide assistance in the aftermath of conflict, most have mandates focused on specific sectoral areas. Those with broader mandates and comprehensive, multisectoral development responsibilities play a central role in supporting countries during reconstruction and development. It is thus key that in their activities, such as joint assessment missions, or in-country coordination arrangements and teams, they assume critical leadership roles in ensuring that gender perspectives are given adequate attention in all areas of reconstruction.

Recommendations

Action 1: Identify and address problems relating to land and property rights facing women returnees, particularly in situations where their husbands are missing.

Action 2: Ensure that the principles of gender equality and non-discrimination are considered during the formulation of constitutions in the post-conflict era; that legal reforms are based on gender analysis of civil and criminal law, in particular in the areas of nationality, property and inheritance, and address criminalization of violence against women and girls, including sexual violence.

Action 3: Promote sensitization of the judiciary on women's human rights to raise their awareness of and capacity to address gender issues.

Action 4:   Address in all support provided to electoral processes the need to ensure the equitable participation of women, through the use of quotas, where relevant; collaborate with local women's groups and networks and support training for women.

Action 5:   Ensure that attention to gender perspectives in economic reconstruction does not only imply micro-credit programmes for women but entails analysis of economic policy-making and planning from a gender perspective and efforts to increase the participation of women in economic decision-making; and incorporate gender perspectives into all support to national budget processes, in line with the outcome of the International Conference on Financing for Development (2002).

Action 6:   Identify and address social and legal barriers to education and employment for women and girls, through both mainstream and targeted interventions.

Action 7:   Ensure in efforts to secure local ownership for reconstruction processes that women's groups and networks are actively involved, particularly at decision-making levels.

Action 8:   Develop clear strategies and action plans (with targets and timetables) on the incorporation of gender perspectives in rehabilitation and reconstruction programmes, including monitoring mechanisms, and the development of targeted activities, with adequate resources, focused on specific constraints facing women and girls in post-conflict situations.

Action 9:   Incorporate attention to the situation of women and girls in conflict and post-conflict situations in needs assessments, initial appraisals and implementation plans for all sectors.

Action 10:   Fully incorporate gender perspectives into the UNDAF process, in particular in the preparation of the Common Country Assessments, the identification of common key indicators and the work of thematic groups.

Action 11:   Ensure that United Nations entities with broad multisectoral mandates and coordination responsibilities, particularly in relation to joint assessments, assume leadership roles in giving attention to gender perspectives in all reconstruction efforts.

VIII. Disarmament, Demobilization and Reintegration

393. Disarmament, demobilization and reintegration (DDR) processes are central components of peace processes and post-conflict environments and can occur with or without the presence of peacekeeping or peace-building missions and with or without the United Nations taking the lead. Ideally, establishment of the parameters of formal DDR processes is part of peace negotiations and is solidified in peace accords.[1]

394. One of the most important goals of disarmament relates to the collection, safe storage and destruction of armaments and ammunition following conflicts. In recent years, national Governments, regional and international organizations have been involved in such disarmament activities, some of which entail the provision of various material incentives – such as community development assistance – to encourage the surrender of such weapons. Such disarmament activities are of great importance to women because of heightened threats to their personal security with the proliferation of weapons in post-conflict situations. For this reason, women and girls are actively involved in weapons collection programmes.

395. In order to be successful, DDR initiatives must be based on a concrete understanding of who combatants are – women, men, girls, boys. Recent analyses of DDR processes from a gender perspective have highlighted that women combatants are often invisible and their needs overlooked. In attempting to understand how and why gender is a relevant dimension in DDR programming, these analyses take up broad issues, such as the definitions and role of masculinity in arms ownership and "demilitarization" processes as well as provide concrete guidance in the form of checklists and questions.[2]

396. Most disarmament, demobilization and reintegration programmes in the past targeted only males above the age of 18 years, who fit the international definitions of soldiers. Questionnaires designed to assess the entry and conditions of ex-combatants into demobilization programmes do not take into account whether the person served in a capacity other than as an armed combatant.[3] This limited notion of who a combatant is poses a problem for all three phases of DDR programming. Although they do not satisfy

most international legal or working definitions of "combatants" or "armed elements", women and children who supported the fighters (willingly or unwillingly) are also in need of demobilization, rehabilitation, and reintegration assistance. Even when they have "joined" fighting forces, women and adolescent girls are often not recognized as combatants and are denied entry into these programmes.[4]

397. While the recognition of women's roles in armed forces and groups remains problematic, the Cape Town Principles, used by UNICEF and other lead agencies, offer a more comprehensive framework for recognizing the roles of child soldiers. The Cape Town Principles define a child soldier as "any person under 18 years of age who is part of any kind of regular or irregular armed force in any capacity, including but not limited to cooks, porters, messengers, and those accompanying such groups, other than purely as family members. It includes girls recruited for sexual purposes and forced into marriage. It does not, therefore, only refer to a child who is carrying or has carried arms".[5] At the same time, many fighting forces and groups do not disclose the presence of child soldiers within their ranks, thus excluding them from formal disarmament processes. In Sierra Leone release of women and children from within the ranks was a condition of the peace agreement. Such developments have resulted in the Secretary-General recommending that parallel plans be developed to document, track and provide support for those child combatants who do not enter formal disarmament, demobilization and reintegration processes.[6]

A. Disarmament

398. Sustainable peace necessitates disarmament because resurgence in violence, increased banditry, and criminal and interpersonal violence can often be attributed to the ready availability of weapons. Formal disarmament processes usually occur following formal peace accords and involve the collection, control and disposal of all weapons including small arms, explosives, and light and heavy weapons of both combatants and civilians. It also includes the development of responsible arms management programmes.[7] At times, material goods, or in some instances cash payments, are made available in an effort to provide incentives for the surrendering of weapons. Disarmament also involves the transport of ex-combatants from opposition groups, and government forces or civil defense militias to encampment areas and discharge centres.

399. As pointed out earlier in the study, women have historically played a key role in lobbying and advocating for disarmament and it is important that women and girls are actively involved in disarmament activities in DDR programmes.

400. As part of building community support for disarmament, consultation with women's groups and women within the community can provide important information regarding perceptions of the dangers posed by the number of weapons, attitudes towards the types and numbers of weapons within the community, information regarding traditional mechanisms to respond to the problem of high numbers of weapons and, potentially, the identification of weapons caches and trans-border weapons trade.[8] Recently, women's and civil society groups have been partners in public campaigns to encourage combatants to lay down their arms, and in collections and public destruction of weapons.[9] Women in Liberia pushed for disarmament as a precursor to elections, while in the eastern Democratic Republic of the Congo women rallied to call for disarmament as a precursor to the opening of peace talks. The "weapons-for-development" project in Albania, jointly managed by the United Nations Department for Disarmament Affairs (DDA) and UNDP, is one successful example for community development assistance in this context.[10] Women in Afghanistan are adamant about the need for all fighting forces to be disarmed. The participation of civil society is essential to ensuring a secure and lasting peace after international peace missions have been withdrawn.[11]

B. Demobilization

401. Demobilization is "the process by which armed forces (Government and/or opposition or factional forces) either downsize or completely disband, as part of a broader transformation from war to peace".[12] Key factors necessary to consider in constructing and managing cantonment sites include maximizing accessibility of sites by centralizing them reasonably near concentrations of ex-combatants; providing adequate security mechanisms to ensure the safety of those within the site; providing basic amenities for shelter, food, water, health care and recreation; properly securing and guarding weapons; and establishing lines of communication to facilitate the exchange of information inside and outside the site.

402. The specific needs of female combatants and women and girls "camp followers" are often not taken into consideration in the design or implementation of the disarmament programmes, as occurred recently in East Timor

and Sierra Leone.[13] In Sierra Leone camps had separate wings for women and girls, which were distant from the men's wings. Women who chose not to register and live in the vicinity of the camps where their "husbands" were located, found themselves in a very vulnerable environment. Key problems concerned their safety and their secure and reliable access to basic provisions, such as water and food.

403. Although, families often accompany ex-combatants to assembly areas and establish temporary residences around cantonment sites, there is, at present, no clear policy regarding these families. Particular areas to be addressed regarding families include family guardianship while ex-combatants are in demobilization exercises, types of support the family will receive, and eligibility criteria for services.[14]

404. During transportation of disarmed ex-combatants to cantonment and encampment sites, women and girls forced to serve as "wives" have had to accompany their captors, as occurred in Mozambique.[15] In Sierra Leone wives were never forced to travel with their captors. Women or children who reported as combatants were processed as female ex-combatants or child soldiers. When women follow men as "camp followers" and settle close to cantonment areas, they become vulnerable as internally displaced persons. Women and girls may face problems regarding protection from former captors. When sexual slavery has been a part of the armed conflict, women and adolescent girls may also be travelling with small children born in captivity. Sites are rarely designed with the basic provisions and protection needs of these populations in mind.

405. In some cases abducted women may be among the last to be relinquished, due to the fact that women and girls are considered the "rewards" and property of their captors and their unpaid labour is valued. In some cases, without adequate international pressure, such women and girls may not be released at all.[16]

406. Demobilization includes a variety of tasks, such as socio-economic surveys and skills inventories; services to ex-combatants with disabilities, those who are chronically ill or in need of psychological care; and support for families of ex-combatants. It should also involve, as integral elements, provision of special measures for women and girl combatants.

407. Since women and adolescent girls are often not recognized as combatants and the wide variety of support roles they have undertaken are not taken into account, discrimination can result throughout the entire demobilization process. This includes the screening process, access to the demobi-

lization certificate/discharge book, receipt of incentives, and the design of cantonment sites and demobilization programmes. In Sierra Leone women and girls were recognized as combatants and registered into the process. Young girls who were non-combatants were recognized as separated children in the company of combatants, and were accepted into the programme and immediately referred to child protection agencies.

408. The widespread abduction of women and girls in conflict situations raises the question of what constitutes a "family". In such cases, abductees need to be recognized and given access to demobilization programmes and benefits in their own right, regardless of the status with their "husband/ father". In Sierra Leone when children referred to themselves as a family of combatants verification procedures were carried out. In some instances, women and girls have been forced against their will to accompany men to demobilization sites. Consequently, the term "camp followers" should be used with caution. In other cases, women and girls were excluded when the men decided to leave them behind, in some cases leaving them standing on the side of the road as the men were driven away to the sites.[17] Government agencies, Save the Children/UK and UNICEF have collaborated on the transport of abducted women and children from southern Sudan to transit care centres near Khartoum where space has been created to enable women and girls to discuss "bush relationships" without intimidation or contact with their "husbands".

409. As is the case with disarmament, incentives to demobilize include financial and material subsidies and benefits, such as food, clothing, shelter, tools, transportation and education. Incentive programmes have routinely favoured men and marginalized or excluded women and girls. At times, this has resulted in women and girls having few economic choices except to stay with their captors who have received money, material goods and training. There are often barriers to women and girls being granted training and resettlement allowances.[18] In East Timor, for example, specific programmes were designed for former Failintil freedom fighters, with those not going into the new East Timor Defence Force receiving a remuneration package for $100 plus language and computer training. Nothing comparable was offered for the women who supported these men throughout the struggle.[19]

410. Demobilization programmes for child soldiers are rare. The few that do exist tend to focus on the needs of boys, largely ignoring the existence and needs of girl soldiers, in spite of the fact that in some countries girls comprise around 40 per cent of all child soldiers. In addition, because of their experiences during conflict and the stigma on women and girls as

"wives" or fighters, especially in situations where they were abducted into these forces, girls may be less likely to come forward to participate in demobilization programmes. With few exceptions, programmes do not to take into full account the experiences of girls in fighting forces and groups, and the resulting economic, social, health and psychological implications.

411. When child soldiers have been excluded from demobilization processes, families and mothers in particular, who had little or no resources, were unofficially expected to handle the demobilization and reintegration process of youth and child soldiers. In Sierra Leone children were placed in interim care centres for at least six weeks and were screened medically and provided with psychosocial counselling. Such children were subsequently registered in long-term educational programmes or vocational skills training.

412. In a welcome initiative, UNICEF, a lead agency for advocacy and programme implementation for child soldiers, has taken a principal role in working to address the needs of girl soldiers by providing technical support to locate and remove girls from adult camps as soon as possible and assisting in the development of national plans aimed at sustainable programmes for girls' demobilization and reintegration.[20] UNICEF also promotes the participation of girls in the design and implementation of disarmament, demobilization and reintegration, vocational training and peer counselling programmes.

C. Reintegration

413. Reintegration programmes are "assistance measures provided to former combatants that would increase the potential for their economic and social reintegration into society".[21] Social reintegration includes the sensitization of communities to assist in reconciliation and help to integrate ex-combatants into the communities. Such community support is necessary to build confidence in ex-combatants' decisions to disarm and demobilize and to ensure sustainable peace. Family reunification also plays an important role in social reintegration. Key actors within these processes include public officials, community elders and leaders of religious organizations and local NGOs. Social reintegration also entails longer-term care of the wounded, disabled, mentally ill and chronically ill ex-combatants, and special programmes for high-risk groups, such as child soldiers, women and girls who have been subjected to sexual abuse or slavery.

414. Short-term activities in social and economic reintegration are numerous and include family reunification services, health counselling, medical care, general education, job counselling and referral, specific measures for vulnerable groups, vocational training and departure packages, which include cash, clothing, food and food coupons, housing and housing materials. These activities are supported and carried out by United Nations departments, programmes and agencies, as well as the ICRC, IOM, bilateral agencies and NGOs. Long-term initiatives for social and economic reintegration include integrated programmes for ex-combatants, credit programmes, land reform and land allocations, professional and vocational training, public works job creation, income-generation programmes, hiring incentives, business and legal advice, and children's programmes. The gender perspectives of these activities need to be identified and concrete strategies developed for addressing them.

415. Economic reintegration presents a major challenge as the local communities are often impoverished by wars and do not have the material or economic capacity to assist ex-combatants. Most economic reintegration programmes are established for and dominated by men, leaving women and girls with limited skills training. With few immediate job opportunities, particularly within the formal sector, women and girls have limited options for economic reintegration, which can have serious implications if they have sole responsibility for dependants. When reintegration programmes do not take account of the dependants of ex-combatants, women and girls may resort to sleeping on the streets or turning to prostitution to survive. Women and girls who have lost husbands also often lack proper financial support and are seldom active participants in reintegration training programmes.

416. The extent to which the briefings, counselling and training in reintegration programmes for the eventual reintegration of ex-combatants take into consideration the differences in women's and girls' experiences of the conflict, as compared to men and boys, is unclear. There is little indication that analyses of what comprise marketable skills and subsequent training and programmes reflect the differences and inequalities in the access of women, girls, men and boys to labour markets, capital, property and investments. Resettlement does not always consider national or customary laws regarding the rights of women and girls to own or dispose of property, including land, or their potential inability to return to family homes if their husband is deceased or missing. However, in Sierra Leone reintegration skills training programmes offer women and men a wide range of skills relevant to the local economy. The National Committee for Disarmament, Demobilization and Reintegration is currently undertaking a

Demobilization and Reintegration is currently undertaking a review of its training programmes so as to provide more relevant skills to all ex-combatants. Education and training programmes rarely provide for child-care, thus impeding the access of women and adolescent girls with dependants to these initiatives.[22]

417. In some cases, women and girls who experienced more egalitarian roles within fighting forces and groups, emerged from conflict into societies which are marked by increased pressure for women and girls to retreat from public life and the formal economy in order to make space for returning male ex-combatants.[23] Women and girls who fought as combatants may also face increased stigmatization within their communities for breaking traditional roles associated with being female. There may be differences in the way the wartime activities of women and men are viewed after the conflict has come to an end.

418. While relationships in the context of armed conflict may have started with abduction and sexual abuse, many of these relationships have been sustained over the years and transformed into family units. In Sierra Leone efforts are made to reach out to women in such situations and to advise them of the options at their disposal. Mechanisms are often not in place to facilitate women and girls making choices about their final reintegration destination after leaving the camp, especially if their views differ from their "husband/father".[24]

419. Programmes that take gender perspectives into consideration are being designed and implemented in a fragmented ad hoc manner and few gender-specific initiatives exist. In Sierra Leone, for example, the only gender-specific programme for adult female ex-combatants is micro-credit. No programmes take into consideration the extensive level of gender and sexual-based violence, lack of reproductive health care, the presence of continued violence from "bush husbands" and the stigma facing survivors of abduction and rape.[25]

420. Local women's and civic groups have provided counselling and guidance to widows, women and girl ex-combatants on gender-specific issues. Women and girls who were subjected to sexual abuse may face particularly high levels of stigmatization and rejection by their communities and families. Some local communities have mobilized around this issue and have worked to sensitize communities on the impact of these actions upon women and girls in order to help ease their reintegration and lessen stigma, as in Mozambique, Sierra Leone and Uganda.

421. Most child soldiers are likely to return to home situations more impoverished than when they left. In Sierra Leone, special programmes facilitated by UNICEF and funded by various donors, provide support to child-headed households in the form of skills training, a small credit revolving fund, and non-formal education on the health of women, child care and HIV/AIDS. For the most part, however, United Nations entities, NGOs and community groups have yet to develop strategies to allow for adequate time frames for reintegration programmes for girls or boys.

422. In Sierra Leone, the Child Protection Adviser works very closely with UNICEF, the National Committee for Disarmament, Demobilization and Reintegration and the child protection agencies, in developing the procedural guidelines for the processing of child combatants, including girls. With the use of the UNAMSIL Trust Fund, the child protection agencies facilitated the development and organization of community-based projects to respond to the needs of girl ex-combatants and separated girls. Grass-roots women's organizations have been assisted to provide services, including the strengthening of sensitization for the community, small credit skills training, informal education for separated girls and survivors of sexual abuse.

423. An important element of reintegration programmes is the understanding of the impact of demobilization and reintegration on domestic life when family relations were strained and broken during the conflict. Women may be pushed out of jobs as preference is given to ex-combatants. If the reintegration of demobilized men is not successful, these men may join gangs and contribute to rising street violence. Domestic violence may increase, and wives may be at risk from STI including HIV/AIDS, passed on by their returning husbands.[26]

Recommendations

Action 1: Incorporate the needs and priorities of women and girls as ex-combatants, "camp-followers" and families of ex-combatants in the design and implementation of DDR programmes, including the design of camps, the distribution of benefits, and access to basic resources and services, including food, water, health care, counselling, in order to ensure the success of such programmes and the participation and full access to benefits for women and girls.

Action 2: Increase the number of programmes for child soldiers and fully incorporate attention to the specific situation and needs of girl soldiers, and identify means to support child soldiers, including girls, who do not enter DDR programmes.

Action 3: Recognize the impact of armed conflict and displacement on family relations and develop awareness of the risks for increased domestic violence, especially in the families of ex-combatants; and develop programmes on the prevention of domestic violence which target families and communities, and especially male ex-combatants.

Action 4: Recognize and utilize the contributions of women and girls in encouraging ex-combatants to lay down arms, in weapons collections programmes and ensure that they benefit from any incentives provided for such activities.

Action 5: Ensure full access of women and girls to all resources and benefits provided in reintegration programmes, including skills development programmes.

Notes

Chapter I

1   Security Council resolutions 1261 (1999), 1265 (1999), 1296 (2000) and 1314 (2000), Presidential Statement S/PRST/2000/7.

2   Statements were made by the Secretary-General, Mr. Kofi Annan, the Special Adviser to the Secretary-General on Gender Issues and the Advancement of Women, Ms. Angela King, and the Executive Director of UNIFEM, Ms. Noeleen Heyzer. Statements by representatives of Member States were, in order of presentation: Jamaica, United States of America, Tunisia, Argentina, China, United Kingdom of Great Britain and Northern Ireland, Bangladesh, Russian Federation, Netherlands, Canada, France, Malaysia, Ukraine, Mozambique, Egypt, Democratic Republic of the Congo, South Africa, Liechtenstein, Singapore, Pakistan, Japan, Cyprus, Republic of Korea, India, New Zealand, Zimbabwe, Indonesia, United Republic of Tanzania, Australia, Croatia, Belarus, Ethiopia, Malawi, Guatemala, United Arab Emirates, Norway, Rwanda, Botswana, Nepal and Namibia.

3   Ambassador Diego Arria of Venezuela conceptualized this type of meeting to enable the members of the Security Council to hear the views of NGOs and others in an informal meeting.

4   *From Beijing to Beijing +5: Review and appraisal of the implementation of the Beijing Platform for Action,* (New York, United Nations, 2001).

5   Report of the Secretary-General on the causes of conflict and the promotion of a durable peace and sustainable development in Africa (A/52/871 – S/1998/318), para. 4.

6   Report of the Expert of the Secretary-General, Ms. Graca Machel. *Impact of armed conflict on children* (A/51/306), para. 24 [hereafter Machel report]; see also Simon Chesterman, ed., *Civilians in War* (Boulder, Lynne Rienner, 2001).

7   International Committee of the Red Cross, *Arms availability and the situation of civilians in armed conflict* (Geneva, 1999).

8   Machel report.

9   Ibid.

[10]   *Report of the Fourth World Conference on Women,* Beijing, 4 to 15 September 1995 (United Nations publication, Sales No. E.96.IV.13), chap. I, resolution 1, annex I and II.

[11]   Chandra Talpade Mohanty, "Cartographies of struggle: Third World women and the politics of feminism", *Third world women and the politics of feminism,* C.T. Mohanty, A. Russo and L. Torres, eds. (Bloomington, Indiana University Press, 1991), p. 29.

[12]   Monica Kathina Juma, Unveiling women as pillars of peace: peace building in communities fractured by conflict in Kenya – an interim report, (Management Development and Governance Division, Bureau for Development Policy, United Nations Development Programme, May 2000), p. 1.

[13]   Pam Ransom, "Reports of panels and presentations: women and peace-building", *Building a Women's Peace Agenda,* Hague Appeal for Peace, ed. (New York, New York Gender Focus Group of the Hague Appeal for Peace, 2001).

[14]   Briefings on Development and Gender Institute of Development Studies, "Conflict and Development" (Sussex, 1996), p. 1; International Committee of the Red Cross, *Women facing war,* (Geneva, 2001).

[15]   Meredeth Turshen and Clotilde Twagiramariya, eds., *What women do in wartime: Gender and conflict in Africa* (London, Zed Books, 1998).

[16]   United Nations Office of the Special Adviser on Gender Issues and Advancement of Women, *Gender mainstreaming: An overview* (New York, United Nations, 2001), p. 1.

[17]   General Assembly resolution 47/226.

[18]   *Women 2000,* "Sexual violence and armed conflict: United Nations response". (United Nations Division for the Advancement of Women, New York, April 1998).

[19]   Report of the Secretary-General on rape and abuse of women in the territory of the former Yugoslavia (E/CN.4/1994/5).

[20]   Report of the Secretary-General pursuant to paragraph 2 of Security Council resolution 808 (1993) (S/25704), Annex, as amended 13 May 1998 [hereafter Statute of the ICTY].

[21]   Security Council resolution 955 (1994), Annex [hereafter Statute of the ICTR].

[22]   *Rome Statute of the International Criminal Court,* United Nations document. A/Conf.183/9 (17 July 1998) [hereafter Statute of the ICC].

[23]   Report of the Secretary-General on the establishment of a Special Court for Sierra Leone, of 4 October 2000 (S/2000/915), annex [hereafter Statute of the Special Court for Sierra Leone].

[24]   General Assembly resolution 48/104.

[25]   General Assembly resolutions S-23/2, annex and S-23/3, annex.

[26]   Preliminary report of the Special Rapporteur on violence against women, its causes and consequences (E/CN.4/1995/42), para. 7.

[27]   Report of the Special Rapporteur on violence against women, its causes and consequences: on violence against women as perpetrated and/or condoned by the State (E/CN.4/1998/54); on violence during times of armed conflict (97 to 2000), (E/CN.4/2001/73).

[28]   Final report of the Special Rapporteur on the situation of systematic rape, sexual slavery and slavery-like practices during periods of armed conflict (E/CN.4/Sub.2/1998/13), para. 6.

[29]   Update to the final report of the Special Rapporteur on the situation of systematic rape, sexual slavery and slavery-like practices during periods of armed conflict (E/CN.4/Sub.2/2000/21).

[30]   Machel report.

[31]   S/PRST/2001/16.

[32]   Report of the Panel on United Nations Peace Operations (A/55/305-S/2000/809); Implementation of the recommendations of the Special Committee on Peacekeeping Operations and the Panel on United Nations Peace Operations (A/55/977).

[33]   S/2000/693.

[34]   S/PRST/2002/6.

Chapter II

[1]   ICRC, *Women Facing War*.

[2]   Coalition to End the Use of Child Soldiers [Coalition], *Child soldiers global report* (London, Coalition, 2001); Coalition, "Americas report", 2000a [Online www.childsoldiers.org/americas]; Coalition, "Africa report", 2000b [Online www.childsoldiers.org/africa]; Coalition, "Asia report", 2000c [Online www.childsoldiers.org/asia]; Coalition, "Europe report", 2000d [Online www.childsoldiers.org/europe]; Coalition, "Special report: Girls with guns", 2000e [Online www.childsoldiers.org/reports]; Dyan Mazurana and others, "Girls in fighting

forces: Their recruitment, participation, demobilization, and reintegration", *Peace & Conflict*, vol. 8, No. 2 (2002), p. 97.

[3] Binta Mansaray, "Women against weapons: A leading role for women in disarmament", *Bound to Cooperate: Conflict, Peace and People in Sierra Leone*. Anatole Ayissi and Robin-Edward Poulton, eds. (Geneva, UNRISD, 2000).

[4] Women's Commission for Refuge Women and Children. *Rwanda's women and children: The long road to reconciliation* (New York, 1997).

[5] Sanam Anderlini, *Women at the peace table: Making a difference* (New York, UNIFEM, 2000).

[6] ICRC, *Women Facing War.*

[7] Ibid.

[8] Amnesty International, *Broken bodies, shattered minds: Torture and ill-treatment of women* (London, 2001). Between 1999-2000 in every case of armed conflict investigated by Amnesty International, there were cases of women and girls being tortured.

[9] *Broken Bodies, Shattered Minds*; Ximena Bunster, "Surviving beyond fear: Women and torture in Latin America", *Surviving beyond fear: Women, children and human rights in Latin America*, Marjorie Agosin, ed. (New York, White Pine Press, 1993), pp. 98-125; Isis-WICCE, *Women's experiences of armed conflict in Uganda, Gulu District 1986 to 1999* (Kampala, 2001); Isis-WICCE "Medical intervention study of war-affected Gulu District, Uganda" (Kampala, 2001).

[10] IASC Secretariat, Mainstreaming gender in the humanitarian response to emergencies, IASC Working Group, XXXVI Meeting, Rome, 22-23 April 1999; *Women facing war*; Report of the Special Representative of the Secretary-General on internally displaced persons (E/CN.4/1996/52); Elizabeth Colson, "War and domestic violence", *Cultural Survival Quarterly,* vol. 19, No. 1 (Spring 1995), p. 38; Cynthia Enloe, *The morning after: Sexual politics at the end of the Cold War* (Berkeley, University of California Press, 1993).

[11] Anderlini, *Women at the peace table.*

[12] Lepa Mladjenovic, "Ethics of difference—Working with women survivors", *Common grounds: Violence against women in war and armed conflict situations*, Indai Lourdes Sajor, ed. (Quezon City, Asian Centre for Women's Human Rights, 1998), p. 355; Zorica Mrsevic and Donna Hughes, "Violence against women in Belgrade, Serbia", *Violence Against Women*, vol. 3, No. 2 (April 1997), p. 101.

13   United Nations Department for Disarmament Affairs, Gender perspectives on disarmament, briefing notes, October 2001.

14   Mary-Wynne Ashford and Yolanda Huet-Vaugn, "The impact of war on women", *War and Public Health*, Barry Levy and Victor Sidel, eds. (Oxford, OUP 1997), pp. 186-196.

15   S. Matthews, "Women in conflict", *Conflict Trends*, vol. 4. (2000)

16   Meredeth Turshen, "Women's war stories". *What women do in wartime: Gender and conflict in Africa*. Meredeth Turshen and Clotilde Twagirarmariya. eds. (London, Zed Books, 1998).

17   CEDAW/C.2001/1/Add.1/; CRC/C/15/Add.133; CRC/C/15/Add.116; A/51/306.

18   Report of the Special Rapporteur on violence against women, its causes and consequences (E/CN.4/2001/73).

19   Ximena Bunster, "Surviving beyond fear"; Jacklyn Cock, *Women and War in South Africa* (London, Open Letters Press, 1993); Alexandra Stiglmayer, ed. *Mass Rape: The War Against Women in Bosnia-Herzegovina* (Lincoln, University of Nebraska Press, 1994).

20   Stiglmayer, *Mass rape.*

21   Stephen Lewis, Special Envoy of the Secretary-General for AIDS in Africa, 21 June 2001, panel discussion.

22   Amnesty International, *Sierra Leone: Rape and other forms of sexual violence against girls and women* (London, 2000); Report of the High Commissioner for Human Rights on the situation of human rights in Sierra Leone (E/CN.4/2001/35).

23   Isis-WICCE, *Women's experiences of armed conflict in Uganda, Gulu District 1986 to 1999*, p. 21.

24   Human Rights Watch, *Leave none to tell the story: Genocide in Rwanda* (New York, 1999).

25   Stiglmayer, *Mass rape.*

26   Kiyoko Furusawa and Jean Inglis, "Violence against women in East Timor under the Indonesian occupation", *Common grounds*, Indai Lourdes Sajor, ed.; Human Rights Watch Africa and Human Rights Watch Women's Rights Project, *Shattered lives: Sexual violence during the Rwandan genocide and its aftermath* (New York, 1996).

27   Coalition, *Child soldiers global report*; A/51/306; Report of the High Commissioner for Human Rights on the situation of human rights in Sierra Leone (E/CN.4/2001/35).

28 Report of the Special Rapporteur on violence against women, its causes and consequences (E/CN.4/2001/73).

29 Note for implementing and operational partners by UNHCR and Save the Children-UK on sexual violence and exploitation: The experience of refugee children in Guinea, Liberia and Sierra Leone (UNHCR-Save Note), (February 2002).

30 "New IOM figures on the global scale of trafficking", *Trafficking in Migrants Quarterly Bulletin*, No. 23 (April 2001).

31 Report of the Special Rapporteur on violence against women, its causes and consequences on trafficking in women, women's migration and violence against women (E/CN.4/2000/68).

32 IOM, "Anti-trafficking programme in Kosovo – through prevention, awareness raising, capacity-building and facilitation", n.d.

33 Amnesty International, "Pakistan: Insufficient protection of women", Amnesty International Index ASA 33/006/2002.

34 Agnes Callamard and others, *Investigating women's rights violations in armed conflicts* (London and Montreal, Amnesty International and the International Centre for Human Rights and Democratic Development, 2001), p. 195.

35 Dyan Mazurana and others, "Girls in fighting forces: Their recruitment, participation, demobilization, and reintegration." *Peace and Conflict*, vol. 8, No. 2, (2002).

36 M. Toole and R.J. Waldman, "Refugees and displaced persons: War, hunger and public health", *Journal of the American Medical Association*, vol. 270 (1993), p. 600.

37 Physicians for Human Rights, *Women's health and human rights in Afghanistan: A population-based assessment* (Boston, 2001).

38 Reiko Watanuki, "The reproductive health of Vietnamese women and chemical weapons", *Common grounds*, Indai Lourdes Sajor ed., pp. 339-348.

39 IASC Secretariat, Mainstreaming Gender in the Humanitarian Response to Emergencies, IASC Working Group, XXXVI Meeting, Rome 22 and 23 April 1999, Final draft background paper; UNFPA, *The impact of conflict on women and girls: A UNFPA Strategy for gender mainstreaming in areas of conflict and reconstruction*", Bratislava, Slovakia, 13-15 November 2001. New York, 2002.

[40] IASC Secretariat, Mainstreaming gender in the humanitarian response to emergencies; Suzanne Williams, *Report of visit to the refugee camps in Macedonia* (Oxfam, UK, April 1999).

[41] Callamard et. al., *Investigating women's rights violations in armed conflicts*; Human Rights Watch, *Leave none to tell the story: Genocide in Rwanda* (New York, 1999); Human Rights Watch Women's Rights Project, "Kosovo: Rape as a weapon of 'ethnic cleansing'", Human Rights Watch report, vol. 12, No. 3 (D), March 2000.

[42] Committee on the Elimination of Discrimination against Women, General Recommendation 15 on avoidance of discrimination against women in national strategies for the prevention and control of AIDS (A/45/38); General Recommendation 24 on Women and health (A/54/38/Rev.1).

[43] United Nations High Commissioner for Refugees, *Sexual violence against refugees* (Geneva, 1995).

[44] R. Fischbach and Herbert, B, "Domestic violence and mental health: Correlates and conundrums within and across cultures", *Social Science Medicine,* vol. 45, No.8 (1997), p. 1161; L. Heise et. al., *Violence against women: The hidden health burden* (Washington, D.C, World Bank, 1994).

[45] Marie de la Soudiere, *The impact of war in the former Yugoslavia: A needs assessment* (Geneva, UNHCR, 1993); Ariane Brunet and Stephanie Rousseau, "Acknowledging violations, struggling against impunity: Women's rights, human rights", *Common grounds,* Indai Lourdes Sajor, ed., pp. 33-60.

[46] International Rescue Committee, *Promoting the rights of children in emergencies: Case study of child and community participation in the IRC's non-formal education and psychosocial support project in Ingushetia* (New York, IRC, 2002), draft.

[47] Coalition, *Child soldiers global report.*

[48] Report of the Secretary-General to the Security Council on the protection of civilians in armed conflict (A/56/259).

[49] Roberta Cohen and Francis M. Deng, *Masses in flight: The global crisis of internal displacement* (Brookings Institution, 1998); E/CN.4/2000/83/Add.1 and E/CN.4/2001/5/Add.3.

[50] Women's Commission for Refugee Women and Children, *Refugee and internally displaced women and children in Serbia and Montenegro* (New York, September 2001).

[51]   See, for example, Isis-WICCE, *Women's experiences of armed conflict in Uganda, Gulu District 1986-1999;* Sue Lautze and others, *Coping with crisis: A review of coping strategies throughout Afghanistan 1999 to 2002* (Washington, D.C., USAID, 2002).

[52]   IASC Secretariat, Mainstreaming gender in the humanitarian response to emergencies.

[53]   Report of the Special Rapporteur on the situation of human rights in Somalia (E/CN.4/1998/96); Brigitte Sørensen, *Women and post-conflict reconstruction: Issues and sources* (Geneva, UNRISD and the Programme for Strategic and International Security Studies, 1998).

[54]   Machel report.

[55]   Craig Cohen and Noah Hendler, *Nta Nzu Itagira Inkigi: No home without foundation: A portrait of child-headed households in Rwanda* (New York, Women's Commission for Refugee Women and Children, 1997).

[56]   Women's Commission for Refugee Women and Children, *Rwanda's Women and Children.*

[57]   Ibid., p. 10.

[58]   Cohen and Hendler, *Nta Nzu Itagira Inkigi: No home without foundation.*

[59]   E/CN.4/1998/96.

[60]   Ibid.

[61]   Lautze, "Coping with crisis".

[62]   Report of the United Nations High Commissioner for Refugees (E/2002/14).

[63]   United Nations High Commissioner for Refugees and Save the Children-UK, "The experience of refugee children in Guinea, Liberia and Sierra Leone based on initial findings and recommendations from assessment mission 22 October-30 November 2001", February 2002.

[64]   Report of the Special Rapporteur on violence against women, its causes and consequences (E/CN.4/2001/73).

[65]   Report of the High Commissioner for Human Rights on systematic rape, sexual slavery and slavery-like practices during armed conflict (E/CN.4/Sub.2/2002/28).

[66]   Note for implementing and operational partners by UNHCR and Save the Children.

[67]   In its Note on resettlement of refugees with special needs, 25 May 1998

(EC/48/SC/CRP.28), para. 8, UNHCR defined "women at risk" as "those refugee women or women of concern to UNHCR who have protection problems and find themselves without the support of traditional protection mechanisms. Special needs of refugee women in such circumstances could derive from persecution as well as from particular hardships sustained either in their country of origin, during their flight, or in their country of refuge."

[68] Human Rights Watch, *World Report 1999* (New York, 1999).

[69] Report of the Special Representative of the Secretary-General on internally displaced persons (E/CN.4/1996/52); Women's Commission for Refugee Women and Children, *Mission report, Kosovo refugees: A humanitarian and human rights emergency in Albania* (New York, n.d.); UNHCR Guidelines on the Protection of Refugee Women, 1995.

[70] Charli R. Carpenter, "Surfacing children: Limitations of genocidal rape discourse", *Human Rights Quarterly,* vol. 22, No. 2 (2000), p. 248.

[71] Report of the Special Representative of the Secretary-General on internally displaced persons (E/CN.4/2000/83/Add.1).

[72] Ibid.; Report of the Special Rapporteur on violence against women, its causes and consequences (E/CN.4/2001/73).

[73] ICRC, *Women facing war.*

[74] See, for example, E/CN.4/1996/52/Add.2, para. 106.

[75] ICRC, *Women facing war,* p. 154.

[76] Ibid, p. 162.

[77] Ibid; Marifran Carlson, "A tragedy and a miracle: Leonor Alonso and the human cost of State terrorism in Argentina", pp. 71-85; Rita Arditti and M. Brinton Lykes, "The disappeared children of Argentina: The work of the grandmothers of Plaza de Mayo", *Surviving Beyond Fear*, pp. 168-175.

[78] Women's Commission for Refugee Women and Children, *Rwanda's women and children.*

[79] Meredeth Turshen, "Women's war stories.

[80] Judy El-Bushra et. al., Gender-sensitive programme design and planning in conflict-affected situations. Research report. (ACORD, January 2002).

Chapter III

[1] Geneva Convention for the Amelioration of the Condition of the Wounded and Sick in Armed Forces in the Field of 12 August 1949 (75 UNTS 31) [hereafter First Geneva Convention]; Geneva Convention for the Amelioration of the Condition of the Wounded, Sick and Shipwrecked Members of Armed Forces at Sea of 12 August 1949 (75 UNTS 85) [hereafter Second Geneva Convention]; Geneva Convention relative to the Protection of Prisoners of War of 12 August 1949 (75 UNTS 135) [hereafter Third Geneva Convention]; Geneva Convention relative to the Protection of Civilian Persons in Time of War of 12 August 1949 (75 UNTS 287) [hereafter Fourth Geneva Convention]; Protocol Additional to the Geneva Conventions of 12 August 1949, and relating to the Protection of Victims of International Armed Conflicts, adopted in 1977 (Protocol I), (1977) (1125 UNTS 3) [hereafter Protocol I] and Protocol Additional to the Geneva Conventions of 12 August 1949, and relating to the Protection of Victims of Non-International Armed Conflicts, adopted in 1977 (Protocol I), (1977) (1125 UNTS 609) [hereafter Protocol II].

[2] See, for example, Art. 5 First and Third Geneva Conventions, Art. 6 Fourth Geneva Convention and Art. 3 Protocol I.

[3] See Art. 4 Fourth Geneva Convention.

[4] See Pt. II Fourth Geneva Convention and see Arts. 68-71 Protocol I (dealing with relief in favour of the civilian population as defined in Art. 50).

[5] See Report to the Economic and Social Council, E/2002/68/Add.1.

[6] *Prosecutor v Delalic and Others*, Case No. IT-96-21, Judgement (16 November 1998) [hereafter *Celebici Judgement*].

[7] Ibid. at paras. 941 and 963.

[8] See, for example, *Prosecutor v Furundzija,* Case No IT-95-17/1, Judgement (10 December 1998) [hereafter *Furundzija Judgement*]; *Prosecutor* v *Nikolic*, First Amended Indictment, Case No IT-94-2 [hereafter *Nikolic Amended indictment*]; *Prosecutor* v *Jankovic and Others*, Case No IT-96-23, Judgement (22 February 2001) (on appeal) [hereafter *Foca Judgement*]; *Prosecutor* v *Kvocka and Others*, Case No IT-98-30/1, Judgement (2 November 2001) (on appeal) [hereafter *Omarska, Keraterm Camps and Trnopolje Judgement*].

[9] See, for example, *Prosecutor v Akayesu*, Case No. ICTR-96-4, Judgement (2 September 1998) [hereafter *Akayesu Judgement*] at paras. 598 and 687. See also *Prosecutor* v *Nyiramasuhuko and Another*, Indictment, Case No ICTR-97-21 [hereafter *Nyiramasuhuko*

Indictment], (charging sexual violence (rape and forced nudity) as a violation of common Art. 3 by way of torture).

[10]   Fernando and Raquel Mejia v Peru, Annual report of the Inter-American Commission on Human Rights, Report No 5/96, Case No. 10.970, 1 March 1996; Case of Aydin v. Turkey (57/1996/676/866), European Court of Human Rights.

[11]   See, for example, *Prosecutor* v *Furundzija*, Case No. IT-95-17/1, Decision of the Trial Chamber on the Preliminary Motion of the Defence, 29 May 1998.

[12]   See the definition of "forced pregnancy" in Art. 7(f) Statute of ICC.

[13]   See *Akayesu Judgement*.

[14]   *Prosecutor* v *Mesuma*, Case No. ICTR-96-13-1 Judgement (27 January 2000) [hereafter *Musema Judgement*].

[15]   See, *Akayesu Judgement*, para 688.

[16]   See Art. 8(2)(c)(ii) Statute of the ICC.

[17]   See Art. 8(2)(e) and (f) Statute of the ICC.

[18]   See Art. 5(a)(i)(ii) & (iii) Statute of the Special Court for Sierra Leone.

[19]   Rape was confirmed as a crime against humanity in Local Control Council Law No. 10 while provided for national level prosecutions of Nazi war criminals who were not tried by the International Military Tribunal (IMT). Furthermore, while the statute of IMT for the Far East also did not explicitly contain a reference to rape, several indictments did include charges of sexual violence as crimes against humanity.

[20]   However, Art. 3 of the Statute of the ICTR differs from Art. 5 Statute of the ICTY in several important respects. First, it expressly includes the requirement that the acts must form part of a "widespread or systematic attack", which is not expressly mentioned in Art. 5 Statute of the ICTY. Secondly, it introduces the requirement that the attacks must be motivated by "national, political, ethnical, racial or religious grounds", which is not required by Art. 5 Statute of the ICTY.

[21]   In the context of the ICTY see, for example, *Prosecutor* v *Meakic and Others*, Indictment as Amended 2 June 1998, Case No. IT-95-4, [hereafter *Omarska Camp Indictment*]; *Nikolic Amended indictment*. In the context of the ICTR see, for example, *Prosecutor* v *Akayesu*, Indictment as amended 17 June 1997, Case No ICTR-96-4-I [hereafter *Akayesu Indictment*]; *Prosecutor* v *Nyiramasuhuko and Another*, Indictment, Case No. ICTR-97-21 [hereafter *Nyiramasuhuko Indictment*]; *Prosecutor* v *Mesuma*, Indictment, Case No. ICTR-96-12 [hereafter *Musema Indictment*]; and *Prosecutor* v *Semanza*, Indictment,

Case No. ICTR-97-20.

[22] See *Foca Judgement* and *Akayesu Judgement*. See also *Mesuma Judgement*.

[23] *Akayesu Indictment*.

[24] *Furundzija Judgement* at para. 175.

[25] See, for example, Art. 5 (f) Statute of ICTY, Art. 3 (f) Statute of ICTR, and Art. 7 (f) of the Statute of ICC.

[26] See, for example, *Nikolic Amended Indictment*.

[27] See, for example, *Prosecutor* v *Karadzic and Another*, Indictment, Case No IT-95-5; *Foca Judgement; Prosecutor* v *Talic*, Indictment, Case No. IT-99-36; *Prosecutor* v *Brdjanin and Another*, Indictment as amended 20 December 1999, Case No. IT-99-36 and *Prosecutor v Tadic,* Case No. IT-94-1-T Judgement (7 May 1997) (the defendant was found guilty of crimes against humanity by way of persecution, based on, *inter alia*, rapes and other forms of sexual violence).

[28] See Art. 7(1)(g) Statute of the ICC.

[29] See Art. 7 para. 2(c) Statute of the ICC for the definition of "[e]nslavement".

[30] By Art. 7 para. (3), for the purposes of the Statute, gender "refers to the two sexes, male and female, within the context of society. The term "gender" does not indicate any meaning different from the above."

[31] Art. II(d) Genocide Convention refers to "[i]mposing measures intended to prevent births within the group."

[32] See Art. 4 Statute of the ICTY and Art. 2 Statute of the ICTR.

[33] *Akayesu Judgement* at paras. 706-707.

[34] *Musema Judgement*. See also the consideration of rape as genocide in the *Furundzija Judgement*, at para. 172.

[35] *Musema Judgement* para. 163.

[36] *Akayesu Judgement* para. 511.

[37] *Akayesu Judgement*, para. 516.

[38] See, for example, "Preparatory Commission of the International Criminal Court, Addendum, Annex III, Elements of Crimes", UN Doc PCNICC/1999/L.5/Rev.1/Add2 (22 December 1999) 5 and "Preparatory Commission of the International Criminal Court, Dis-

cussion Paper Proposed by the Coordinator", UN Doc PCNICC/2000/WGEC/RT.1 (24 March 2000) 2.

[39] See Art. 22 Statute of the ICTY and Art. 21 Statute of the ICTR.

[40] See Rule 96 Rules of Procedure and Evidence of the International Criminal Tribunal for the former Yugoslavia, adopted 11 February 1994, as amended [hereafter Rules of Procedure and Evidence of the ICTY] and Rule 75 Rules of Procedure and Evidence of the International Criminal Tribunal for Rwanda, adopted on 29 June 1995 as amended [hereafter Rules of Procedure and Evidence of the ICTR].

[41] See Rule 34 Rules of Procedure and Evidence of the ICTY and Rule 34 Statute of the ICTR.

[42] See Rule 34B Rules of Procedure and Evidence of the ICTY and Rule 34B Rules of Procedure and Evidence of ICTR.

[43] See Art. 21(3) Statute of the ICC.

[44] The first session of the Assembly of States Parties adopted a resolution which requires that each State party vote for at least six women and men candidates in the election of judges.

[45] See Arts. 36(8)(a)(iii), 36(8)(b), 42(9) & 44(2), Statute of the ICC. Art. 15 of the Statute of the Special Court for Sierra Leone mandates the appointment of persons with gender expertise in the Office of the Prosecutor.

[46] See Art. 43 Statute of the ICC and see also Art. 16 Statute of the Special Court for Sierra Leone.

[47] See Art. 64(2) Statute of the ICC. The Statute allows the Trial Chamber to "[p]rovide for the protection of the accused, witnesses and victims ...", see Art. 64(6)(e). Provision is made for trials to be held in closed session in certain circumstances, see Arts. 64(7) and 68.

[48] See Art. 68(1) Statute of the ICC. There have been a number of progressive rules relating to evidence in cases of sexual violence, see in particular Rule 96 of the ICTY and ICTR Rules of Procedure and Evidence and Rules 70-73 of the ICC Rules of Procedure and Evidence.

[49] See Art. 68(3) Statute of the ICC.

[50] As part of the settlement of the Persian Gulf conflict (1990-91) the UN Security Council established a Fund to pay compensation for "any direct loss, damage ... or injury to foreign governments, nationals and corporations, as a result of the unlawful invasion and occupation

of Kuwait by Iraq". The fund is administered by the UNCC which functions as a subsidiary organ of the Security Council, para.16 of Security Council resolution 687 (1991).

[51]   See Report and recommendations made by the Panel of Commissioners concerning individual claims for serious personal injury or death (Category "B" claims) (S/AC.26/1994/1); Report and recommendations made by the Panel of Commissioners concerning the first installment of individual claims for damages up to US$100,000 (Category "C" claims) (S/AC.26/1994/3); and "Report and recommendations made by the Panel of Commissioners concerning part one of the first installment of individual claims for damages above US$100,000.00 (Category "D" claims) (S/AC.26/1998/1).

[52]   Art. 24(3) Statute of the ICTY and Art. 23(3) Statute of the ICTR.

[53]   See, for example, "UNHCR policy on refugee women" (1990), "Guidelines on the protection of refugee women" (UNHCR, July 1991); "UNHCR policy on refugee children" (October 1993); "Refugee children: Guidelines on protection and care" (1994); "Sexual violence against refugees: Guidelines on prevention and response" (Guidelines on sexual violence) (UNHCR, 1995); and *Reproductive health in refugee situations: An interagency field manual* (UNFPA, UNHCR, WHO, 1999).

[54]   The United Nations Human Rights Committee has determined, for example, that, "In general, the rights set forth in the [International] Covenant [on Civil and Political Rights] apply to everyone, ... irrespective of his or her nationality or Statelessness. Thus, the general rule is that each one of the rights must be guaranteed without discrimination between citizens and aliens." (General comment No. 15 (1986), paras. 1-2). The Committee has also found that the norms of equality before the law and non-discriminatory, equal protection of the law govern "the exercise of all rights, whether protected under the Covenant or not, which the State party confers by law on individuals within its territory or under its jurisdiction...". (General comment No. 23, para. 4. General comments adopted by the Human Rights Committee, Nos. 1-23, reprinted in Note by the Secretariat, Compilation of general comments and general recommendations adopted by Human Rights Treaty Bodies, United Nations doc. No. HRI/GEN/1/Rev.1, 29 July 1994. Accord, id. No. 18, para. 12. Emphasis added.)

[55]   UNHCR, General conclusion on international protection, No. 79 (XLVII), 1996, para. o; UNHCR, Executive Committee conclusion No 39 (XXXVI) 1985, para. k .

[56]   Article 9 of UNHCR's Statute recognizes that in addition to working with refugees, the organization may "engage in such activities ... as the General Assembly may determine ..." GA resolution 48/116 (1993) set out important criteria for UNHCR's involvement with internally displaced persons.

57   The Guiding principles on internal displacement, E/CN.4/1998/53/Add.2.

58   See, for example, *Prosecutor v Delalic and Others*, Case No IT-96-21, Judgement (16 November 1998).

Chapter IV

1   Brigitte Sørensen, *Women and post-conflict reconstruction: Issues and sources*; Dyan Mazurana and Susan R. McKay, "*Women and peace-building*", *Essays on human rights and democratic development*, vol. No. 8 (Montreal, International Centre for Human Rights and Democratic Development, 1999).

2   Report of the Secretary-General, "*An agenda for peace*" (A/47/277-S/24111).

3   United Nations Department for Disarmament Affairs, Gender perspectives on Disarmament, Briefing notes.

4   Binta Mansaray, "Women against weapons: A leading role for women in disarmament".

5   Brigitte Sørensen, *Women and post-conflict reconstruction*.

6   Ibid.

7   Anderlini, *Women at the peace table.*

8   Shelley Anderson, *Women's many roles in reconciliation,* People Building Peace: European Platform for Conflict Prevention and Transformation, n.d. cited 3 January 2002. [www.oneworld.org/euconflict/pbp/4/2_intro.htm]; Kumudini Samuel, "Gender difference in conflict resolution: The case of Sri Lanka", *Gender, Peace and Conflict,* Inger Skjelsbæk and Dan Smith, eds., (London, Sage Publications, 2001), p. 198.

9   Report of the Special Representative on the human rights situation in Rwanda (E/CN.4/2000/41) para. 183.

10   Susan McKay and Dyan Mazurana, *Raising women's voices for peace-building* (London, International Alert, 2001).

11   International Fellowship of Reconciliation, *Women lead the way to peace* (Alkmaar, Netherlands, 1999).

12   Cockburn, *The space between us,* p. 169; Simona Sharoni, *Gender and the Israeli-Palestinian conflict: The politics of women's resistance* (Syracuse, Syracuse University Press, 1995), p. 112.

[13]   International Alert, *Gender and conflict early warning: A framework for action*, (London, 2002).

[14]   The Canadian Department of Foreign Affairs and International Trade (DFAIT) and the UK Department for International Development (DFID), Gender and Peace Support Operations, "Gender and the conflict phase, presentation outline", Section 4/Facilitator Guide, p. 10.

[15]   International Alert, *Implementing the United Nations Security Council resolution on women, peace and security: Integrating gender into early warning systems*, Report on 1st Expert Consultative Meeting, 7 May 2001, Nairobi, Kenya.

[16]   A/55/985 – S/2001/574.

[17]   Ibid., para. 132;

[18]   Kemi Ogunsanya and Kwezi Mngqibisa, "A gender perspective for conflict management", ACORD Occasional paper No. 4, 2000, p. 3.

[19]   Example provided by the Mano River Women's Network for Peace.

[20]   A/50/60-S/1995/1, paras. 66, 67 and 70.

[21]   Ibid; Machel report.

[22]   Eric Hoskins, "Public health and the Persian Gulf war", *War and Public Health*, Barry Levy and Victor Sidel, eds., (Oxford, Oxford University Press, 1997), pp. 254-280.

[23]   Eva Irene Tuft, "Integrating a gender perspective in conflict resolution: The Colombian case", *Gender, Peace and Conflict*, Inger Skjelsbæk and Dan Smith, eds. (London, Sage Publications, 2001).

[24]   United Nations Research Institute for Social Development (UNRISD), *Rebuilding war-torn societies: Report of the Working Seminar at Cartigny, Geneva, 29 November – 1 December 1993* (Geneva, September 1993).

[25]   Executive Committee of the High Commissioner's Programme, "Refugee women and mainstreaming a gender equality perspective, EC/51/SC/CRP.17

[26]   Sørensen, *Women and post-conflict reconstruction*; Sharoni, *Gender and the Israeli-Palestinian conflict*.

27   Sanam Anderlini, "Women, peace and security: A policy audit from the Beijing Platform for Action to United Nations Security Council resolution 1325 and beyond", (London, International Alert, 2001).

28   Luz Mendez, General Coordinator of Union Nacional de Mujeres Guatemaltecas, Arria Formula Meeting on women, peace and security, 23 October 2000.

29   International Fellowship of Reconciliation, *Women lead the way to peace.*

30   E. Naslund, "Looking at peace through women's eyes: Gender-based discrimination in the Salvadoran peace process", *Journal of Public and International Affairs*, vol. 10 (1999), p. 30.

31   Kvinna till Kvinna, "Engendering the peace process: A gender approach to Dayton and Beyond", (Stockholm, 2000).

32   Louise Olsson, "Gender mainstreaming in practice: The United Nations Transitional Assistance Group in Namibia, " *Women and International Peacekeeping*, Louise Olsson and Torunn Tryggestad, eds. (London, Frank Cass Publishers, 2001), p. 100.

33   Statement by the President of the Security Council, 20 February 2001, (S/PRST/2001/5).

34   CIDA, *Gender equality and peace-building: An operational framework.* Ottawa.

35   United Nations Report of the Secretary-General, *Supplement to an agenda for peace: Position paper of the Secretary-General on the Occasion of the Fiftieth Anniversary of the United Nations*, January 1995, A/50/60-S/1995/1, para. 26; A/55/985-S/2001/574, para. 74.

36   United Nations, "Plan of action on peace-building", para. 7.

37   United Nations Department of Political Affairs and United Nations Development Programme, "Report of the Joint Review Mission on the United Nations post-conflict peace-building support offices", 20 July 2001, p. 11.

38   Cynthia Cockburn et. al., *Women organizing for change: A study of women's local integrative organizations and the pursuit of democracy in Bosnia-Herzegovina*, (Sarajevo, Medica Zenica, June 2001), p. 141.

39   International Fellowship of Reconciliation, "Women and peacemaking: Lessons learned from the Women's Peacemakers Programme", (The Netherlands, International Fellowship of Reconciliation, 2002).

40   Ibid.

41   International Alert, *Integrating gender into early warning systems.*

Chapter V

1   United Nations Department of Peacekeeping Operations, *General guidelines for peace-keeping operations* (New York, United Nations, 1995), UN/210/TC/GG95, chap. 4.

2   Cockburn, *The spaces between us*; Cynthia Cockburn and Dubravka Zarkov, eds., *The post-war moment: Militaries, masculinities and international peacekeeping – Bosnia and the Netherlands*; Office of the Adviser for the Promotion of Equality, East Timor Public Administration, UNTAET, Women in East Timor: A report on women's health, education, economic empowerment and decision-making, April 2002.

3   Recommendations of the Special Committee on Peacekeeping Operations and the Panel on United Nations Peace Operations (A/55/977), annex C.

4   A/55/305-S/2000/809. para 132.

5   Cynthia Cockburn and Dubravka Zarkov, eds., *The post-war moment: Militaries, masculinities and international peacekeeping – Bosnia and the Netherlands* (London, Lawrence and Wishart, 2002).

6   Heidi Hudson, "Mainstreaming gender in peacekeeping operations: Can Africa learn from international experience", *African Security Review*, vol. 9, No. 4 (2000), p. 4.; Gerard J. DeGroot, "A Few Good Women: Gender stereotypes, the military and peacekeeping." *International Peacekeeping*, vol 8, No. 2 (Summer 2001), pp. 23-38.

7   Report of the Special Rapporteur on violence against women, its causes and consequences (E/CN.4/2001/73), para. 58-62.

8   Kristin Astgeirsdottir, "Women, adolescent girls, and girl children in Kosovo: The effect of armed conflict on the lives of women", *The impact of conflict on women and girls: A UNFPA strategy for gender mainstreaming in areas of conflict and reconstruction, Bratislava, Slovakia 13-15 November 2001*. UNFPA, New York, 2002.

9   A/56/472, para. 46.

10   Report of the Secretary-General on the improvement of the status of women in the United Nations system, (A/56/472), para. 45.

11   The *Ten Rules Code of Personal Conduct for Blue Helmets* is available at www.un.org/Depts/dpko/training/Training%20Material/Training_Material_main.htm.

[12] E/CN.4/2001/73, para. 58-62.

[13] Kien Serey Phal, "The lessons of the UNTAC experience and the ongoing responsibilities of the international community for peace-building and development in Cambodia", *Pacifica Review,* 7(2), October/November 1995, p. 132.

[14] United Nations Population Fund, "The impact of conflict on women; Machel report; Natalia Lupi, "Report by the enquiry commission on the behaviour of Italian peacekeeping troops in Somalia", *Yearbook of International Humanitarian Law,* vol. 1 (1998), p. 375.

[15] The SOFA is based on a 1990 model, A/54/594, 1990 and the relevant paragraph is 47(b); the Contribution Agreement is based on A/46/185, 1991, and the relevant sections are paragraphs 5 and 8.

Chapter VI

[1] Joanna Macrae, *Aiding recovery? The crisis of aid in chronic political emergencies,* (London, Zed Books, 2001).

[2] Report of the Secretary-General on strengthening the coordination of emergency humanitarian assistance of the United Nations (A/56/95-E/2001/85).

[3] Ibid.; Report of the Secretary-General to the Security-Council on the protection of civilians in armed conflict (A/56/259).

[4] A/56/259.

[5] Ibid.

[6] See, in particular, Security Council resolutions 1261 (1999), 1265 (1999), 1296 (2000), 1314 (2000) and 1325 (2000) and the Aide-Memoire, which identifies 13 core objectives for protecting civilians in conflict situations (S/PRST/2002/6).

[7] IASC Secretariat, Mainstreaming gender in the humanitarian response to emergencies, p. 8.

[8] NUPI-Fafo, *Gendering human security: From marginalization to the integration of women in peace-building* (Norway, 2001).

[9] UNHCR, Respect our rights: Partnership for equality. Report on the dialogue with refugee women, Geneva, Switzerland 20-22 June 2001 (Geneva, 2001); UNHCR, Prevention and response to sexual and gender-based violence in refugee situations, Conference on sexual and gender-based violence, Geneva 27-29 March 2001 (Geneva, 2001).

[10]   IASC Secretariat, Mainstreaming gender in the humanitarian response to emergencies.

[11]   The Reference Group is co-chaired by UNICEF and WFP. Its participants are FAO, ICRC, IFRC, ICVA, InterAction, IOM, OCHA, OHCHR, SCHR, UNDP, UNFPA, UNHCR and WHO.

[12]   www.reliefweb.int/library

[13]   *Reproductive health in refugee situations: An inter-agency field manual* (Geneva, UNHCR, UNFPA, WHO, 1999).

[14]   The resource kit and all its relevant documents are available at www.reliefweb.int/library/GHARkit. The resource kit includes a number of evaluative documents on this issue.

[15]   See also Jeanne Ward, *If not now, when? Addressing gender-based violence in refugee, internally displaced, and post-conflict settings: A global overview*, (New York: The Reproductive Health for Refugee Consortium, 2002).

[16]   Women's Commission for Refugee Women and Children, *UNHCR policy on refugee women* and guidelines on their protection: An assessment of ten years of implementation (New York, 2002).

[17]   Ibid.

[18]   Inter-Agency Standing Committee, "Report of the Task Force on protection from sexual exploitation and abuse in humanitarian crises", 13 June 2002.

[19]   UNICEF, *The gender dimensions of internal displacement: Concept paper and annotated bibliography*, Office of emergency programmes working paper series (New York, 1998).

Chapter VII

[1]   Chris Corrin, *Gender audit of reconstruction programmes in South Eastern Europe* (Fairfax, California and New York, The Urgent Action Fund and the Women's Commission for Refugee Women and Children, June 2000).

[2]   *Human development report. Deepening democracy in a fragmented world*, (New York/Oxford, Oxford University Press, 2002), p. 4.

[3]   N. Gasa, "National machinery for gender equality", *Democracy and deep-rooted conflict: Options for negotiators*, P. Harris and B. Reilly, eds. (Stockholm, IDEA, 1998), p. 320.

[4]   Ruth Iyob, "The Eritrean experiment: A cautious pragmatism?" *Journal of Modern Afri-*

can Studies, vol. 35, No. 4, p. 647; Sørensen, *Women and post-conflict reconstruction.*

[5]   Corrin, *Gender audit of reconstruction programmes in South Eastern Europe.* p. 6.

[6]   Callamard et. al., Investigating women's rights violations in armed conflicts, p. 198.

[7]   Turshen, "Women's war stories".

[8]   Brunet and Rousseau, "Acknowledging violations, struggling against impunity"; Beth Goldblatt and Sheila Meintjes, "South African Women Demand the Truth", *What women do in wartime*, pp. 55-57.

[9]   Ketty Lazaris, "The role of women's non-governmental organizations in rehabilitation, reconstruction and reconciliation". *The impact of conflict on women and girls: A UNFPA strategy for gender mainstreaming in areas of conflict and reconstruction, Bratislava, Slovakia 13-15 November 2001.* UNFPA, New York, 2002.

[10] Kristin Astgeirsdottir, "Women and girls in Kosovo".

[11] Sørensen, *Women and post-conflict reconstruction.*

[12] Tracy Fitzsimmons, "Engendering a new police identity?" *Peace Review,* vol. 10, No. 2 (1998), p. 274.

[13] Lorraine Corner, *Women, men and economics: The Gender-differentiated impact of macroeconomics* (New York, UNIFEM, 1996); Noeleen Heyzer et. al., eds., *A commitment to the wforld's women: Perspectives on development for Beijing and beyond* (New York, UNIFEM, 1995).

[14] Ibid.; Macrae, *Aiding recovery? The crisis of aid in chronic political emergencies;* Office of the Advisor for the Promotion of Equality, East Timor Public Administration, *Women in East Timor: A Report on women's health, education, economic empowerment and decision-making* (New York, United Nations, April 2002).

[15] Macrae, *Aiding recovery? The crisis of aid in chronic political emergencies.*

[16] Office of the Adviser for the Promotion of Equality, East Timor Public Administration, Women in East Timor: A report on women's health, education, economic empowerment and decision-making.

[17] Sørensen, *Women and post-conflict reconstruction.*

[18] Ibid., p. 32.

[19] See, for example, Human Rights Watch Africa and Human Rights Watch Women's Rights Project, *ShatteredlLives: Sexual violence during the Rwandan genocide and its aftermath* (New York, 1996).

[20] Sørensen, *Women and post-conflict reconstruction,* p. 32.

[21] Virginia Garrard-Burnett, "Aftermath: Women and gender issues in post-conflict Guatemala", Working Paper No. 311, Centre for Development Information and Evaluation (Washington, D.C., U.S. Agency for International Development, September 2000).

[22] Erica Abreha, Annual report, ERT4: Seraye Credit and Savings Scheme - Towards sustainability? (Asmara, ACORD, 1996); Maria Julia, "Revisiting a repopulated village: A step backwards in the changing status of women", *International Social Work,* vol. 38 (1995), pp. 229-242.

[23] See, for example, Garrard-Burnett, "Aftermath: Women and gender issues in post-conflict Guatemala"; Lynn Stephen, Serena Cosgrove, and Kelley Ready, "Aftermath: Women's organizations in post-conflict El Salvador", Working Paper No. 309, Centre for Development Information and Evaluation (Washington, D.C., U.S. Agency for International Development, October 2000); Martha Walsh, "Aftermath: The impact of conflict on women in Bosnia and Herzegovina", Working Paper No. 302, Centre for Development Information and Evaluation (Washington, D.C., U.S. Agency for International Development, July 2000); Martha Walsh, "Aftermath: The role of women's organization in post-conflict Bosnia and Herzegovina", Working Paper No. 308, Centre for Development Information and Evaluation (Washington, D.C., U.S. Agency for International Development, July 2000).

[24] Levy and Sidel, eds., *War and public health.* pp. 137-148.

[25] See, for example, Isis-WICCE, *Women's experiences of armed conflict in Uganda, Gulu District 1986-1999;* Physicians for human rights, *War-related sexual violence in Sierra Leone.*

[26] Sørensen, *Women and post-conflict reconstruction.*

[27] See, for example, Julie A. Mertus, *War's offensive on women: The humanitarian challenge in Bosnia, Kosovo, and Afghanistan.* (Bloomfield, Connecticut, USA, Kumarian Press, 2000) pp, 32-33.

[28] Machel report; Sørensen, *Women and post-conflict reconstruction.*

[29] Ibid.

30   Women's Commission for Refugee Women and Children, *Rwanda's women and children.*

31   See, for example, Isis-WICCE, Women's experiences of armed conflict in Uganda, Gulu District 1986-1999.

32   Carol Watson, *The flight, exile and return of Chadian refugees: A case study with a special focus on women* (Geneva, UNRISD, 1996).

33   Women's Commission for Refugee Women and Children, Rights, reconstruction and enduring peace: Afghan women and children after the Taliban (New York, December 2001), p. 5.

34   Julie A. Mertus, *War's offensive on women*, pp. 32-33.

Chapter VIII

1   United Nations Department of Peacekeeping Operations, *Disarmament, demobilization and reintegration of ex-combatants in a peacekeeping environment: Principles and guidelines* (New York, December 1999).

2   See, for example, Nathalie de Watteville, *Addressing gender issues in demobilization and reintegration programmes.* Africa Region Working Paper Series (Washington, The World Bank, 2002); Vanessa Farr, Gendering demilitarization as a peace-building tool. (Bonn, Bonn International Centre for Conversion, 2002).

3   United Nations Department of Peacekeeping Operations, *Disarmament, demobilization and reintegration*; see, for example, the screening questionnaire for persons at Lungi Demobilization Centre, Sierra Leone, pp. 104-110.

4   See, for example, Office of the Adviser for the Promotion of Equality, East Timor Public Administration, UNTAET, *Women in East Timor: A report on women's health, education, economic empowerment and decision-making.*

5   UNICEF, Cape Town Annotated Principles and Best Practices. Adopted by the participants in the Symposium on the Prevention of Recruitment of Children into the Armed Forces and Demobilization and Social Reintegration of Child Soldiers in Africa, organized by UNICEF in cooperation with the NGO Sub-group of the NGO Working Group on the Convention on the Rights of the Child, Cape Town (New York, 30 April 1997).

6   Report of the Secretary-General on the role of United Nations peacekeeping in disarmament, demobilization and reintegration (S/2000/101).

7   Ibid., p. 15.

8   See, for example, the efforts of women in Sierra Leone in Mansaray, "Women against weapons".

9   Anderlini, *Women at the peace table;* Machel report.

10 United Nations press release "UN pilot project for weapons collections in Albania holds first meeting",DC/2626, 29 January 1999.

11 United Nations Executive Committee on Humanitarian Affairs (ECHA) Working Group on Disarmament, Demobilization, and Reintegration, "Harnessing institutional capacities in support of disarmament, demobilization and reintegration of former combatants".

12 United Nations Department of Peacekeeping Operations, *Disarmament, demobilization and reintegration.*

13 Women's Commission for Refugee Women and Children, *Disarmament, demobilization and reintegration: Assessing gaps in policy and protection in Sierra Leone for war-affected children and adolescents;* Office of the Adviser for the Promotion of Equality, East Timor Public Administration, *Women in East Timor: A report on women's health, education, economic empowerment and decision-making.*

14 Ibid.

15 Carol Thompson. "Beyond civil society: Child soldiers as citizens in Mozambique." Review of African Political Economy, vol. 80, (1999) p.191; Women's Commission for Refugee Women and Children, *Disarmament, demobilization and reintegration: Assessing gaps in policy and protection in Sierra Leone for war-affected children and adolescents* (New York, 2002), draft.

16 Mazurana et. al., "Girls in fighting forces"; UNICEF Liberia and the U.S. National Committee for UNICEF, *The Disarmament, demobilization and reintegration of child soldiers in Liberia, 1994-1997: The process and lessons learned* (New York, March 1998).

17 Thompson, "Beyond civil society: Child soldiers as citizens in Mozambique".

18 Ibid.; UNICEF Eastern and Southern Africa Regional Office, Inter-agency meeting on demobilization of child soldiers in active combat, Nairobi 10-12 October 2001 (New York, 2001).

19   Office of the Adviser for the Promotion of Equality, East Timor Public Administration, *Women in East Timor: A report on women's health, education, economic empowerment and decision-making.*

20   UNICEF Eastern and Southern Africa Regional Office, Inter-agency meeting on demobilization of child soldiers in active combat, Nairobi 10-12 October 2001.

21   United Nations Department of Peacekeeping Operations, *Disarmament, demobilization and reintegration.*

22   Sørensen, *Women and post-conflict reconstruction.*

23   Ibid.

24   UNICEF Eastern and Southern Africa Regional Office, Inter-agency meeting on demobilization of child soldiers in active combat, Nairobi 10-12 October 2001.

25   Women's Commission for Refugee Women and Children, *Disarmament, demobilization and reintegration: Assessing gaps in policy and protection in Sierra Leone for war-affected children and adolescents;* Physicians for human rights, *War-related sexual violence in Sierra Leone.*

26   Nathalie de Watteville, *Addressing gender issues in demobilization and reintegration programmes.* Africa Region Working Paper Series (Washington, The World Bank, 2002).

Annex

Resolution 1325 (2000)
Adopted by the Security Council at its 4213th meeting
on 31 October 2000

The Security Council,

Recalling its resolutions 1261 (1999) of 25 August 1999, 1265 (1999) of 17 September 1999, 1296 (2000) of 19 April 2000 and 1314 (2000) of 11 August 2000, as well as relevant statements of its President, and *recalling also* the statement of its President to the press on the occasion of the United Nations Day for Women's Rights and International Peace 8 March 2000 (SC/6816),

Recalling also the commitments of the Beijing Declaration and Platform for Action (A/52/231) as well as those contained in the outcome document of the twenty-third Special Session of the United Nations General Assembly entitled "Women 2000: Gender Equality, Development and Peace for the Twenty-First Century" (A/S-23/10/Rev.1), in particular those concerning women and armed conflict,

Bearing in mind the purposes and principles of the Charter of the United Nations and the primary responsibility of the Security Council under the Charter for the maintenance of international peace and security,

Expressing concern that civilians, particularly women and children, account for the vast majority of those adversely affected by armed conflict, including as refugees and internally displaced persons, and increasingly are targeted by combatants and armed elements, and *recognizing* the consequent impact this has on durable peace and reconciliation,

Reaffirming the important role of women in the prevention and resolution of conflicts and in peace-building, and *stressing* the importance of their equal participation and full involvement in all efforts for the maintenance and promotion of peace and security, and the need to increase their role in decision-making with regard to conflict prevention and resolution,

Reaffirming also the need to implement fully international humanitarian and human rights law that protects the rights of women and girls during and after conflicts,

Emphasizing the need for all parties to ensure that mine clearance and mine awareness programmes take into account the special needs of women and girls,

Recognizing the urgent need to mainstream a gender perspective into peacekeeping operations, and in this regard *noting* the Windhoek Declaration and the Namibia Plan of Action on Mainstreaming a Gender Perspective in Multidimensional Peace Support Operations (S/2000/693),

Recognizing also the importance of the recommendation contained in the statement of its President to the press of 8 March 2000 for specialized training for all peacekeeping personnel on the protection, special needs and human rights of women and children in conflict situations,

Recognizing that an understanding of the impact of armed conflict on women and girls, effective institutional arrangements to guarantee their protection and full participation in the peace process can significantly contribute to the maintenance and promotion of international peace and security,

Noting the need to consolidate data on the impact of armed conflict on women and girls,

1. *Urges* Member States to ensure increased representation of women at all decision-making levels in national, regional and international institutions and mechanisms for the prevention, management, and resolution of conflict;

2. *Encourages* the Secretary-General to implement his strategic plan of action (A/49/587) calling for an increase in the participation of women at decision-making levels in conflict resolution and peace processes;

3. *Urges* the Secretary-General to appoint more women as special representatives and envoys to pursue good offices on his behalf, and in this regard *calls on* Member States to provide candidates to the Secretary-General, for inclusion in a regularly updated centralized roster;

4. *Further urges* the Secretary-General to seek to expand the role and contribution of women in United Nations field-based operations, and especially among military observers, civilian police, human rights and humanitarian personnel;

5. *Expresses* its willingness to incorporate a gender perspective into peacekeeping operations, and *urges* the Secretary-General to ensure that, where appropriate, field operations include a gender component;

6. *Requests* the Secretary-General to provide to Member States training guidelines and materials on the protection, rights and the particular

needs of women, as well as on the importance of involving women in all peacekeeping and peace-building measures, *invites* Member States to incorporate these elements as well as HIV/AIDS awareness training into their national training programmes for military and civilian police personnel in preparation for deployment, and *further requests* the Secretary-General to ensure that civilian personnel of peacekeeping operations receive similar training;

7.   *Urges* Member States to increase their voluntary financial, technical and logistical support for gender-sensitive training efforts, including those undertaken by relevant funds and programmes, inter alia, the United Nations Fund for Women and United Nations Children's Fund, and by the Office of the United Nations High Commissioner for Refugees and other relevant bodies;

8.   *Calls on* all actors involved, when negotiating and implementing peace agreements, to adopt a gender perspective, including, inter alia:

(a)   The special needs of women and girls during repatriation and resettlement and for rehabilitation, reintegration and post-conflict reconstruction;

(b)   Measures that support local women's peace initiatives and indigenous processes for conflict resolution, and that involve women in all of the implementation mechanisms of the peace agreements;

(c)   Measures that ensure the protection of and respect for human rights of women and girls, particularly as they relate to the constitution, the electoral system, the police and the judiciary;

9.   *Calls upon* all parties to armed conflict to respect fully international law applicable to the rights and protection of women and girls, especially as civilians, in particular the obligations applicable to them under the Geneva Conventions of 1949 and the Additional Protocols thereto of 1977, the Refugee Convention of 1951 and the Protocol thereto of 1967, the Convention on the Elimination of All Forms of Discrimination against Women of 1979 and the Optional Protocol thereto of 1999 and the United Nations Convention on the Rights of the Child of 1989 and the two Optional Protocols thereto of 25 May 2000, and to bear in mind the relevant provisions of the Rome Statute of the International Criminal Court;

10.   *Calls on* all parties to armed conflict to take special measures to protect women and girls from gender-based violence, particularly rape and other forms of sexual abuse, and all other forms of violence in situations of armed conflict;

11.   *Emphasizes* the responsibility of all States to put an end to impunity and to prosecute those responsible for genocide, crimes against humanity, and war crimes including those relating to sexual and other

violence against women and girls, and in this regard *stresses* the need to exclude these crimes, where feasible from amnesty provisions;

12. *Calls upon* all parties to armed conflict to respect the civilian and humanitarian character of refugee camps and settlements, and to take into account the particular needs of women and girls, including in their design, and recalls its resolutions 1208 (1998) of 19 November 1998 and 1296 (2000) of 19 April 2000;

13. *Encourages* all those involved in the planning for disarmament, demobilization and reintegration to consider the different needs of female and male ex-combatants and to take into account the needs of their dependants;

14. *Reaffirms* its readiness, whenever measures are adopted under Article 41 of the Charter of the United Nations, to give consideration to their potential impact on the civilian population, bearing in mind the special needs of women and girls, in order to consider appropriate humanitarian exemptions;

15. *Expresses* its willingness to ensure that Security Council missions take into account gender considerations and the rights of women, including through consultation with local and international women's groups;

16. *Invites* the Secretary-General to carry out a study on the impact of armed conflict on women and girls, the role of women in peace-building and the gender dimensions of peace processes and conflict resolution, and *further invites* him to submit a report to the Security Council on the results of this study and to make this available to all Member States of the United Nations;

17. *Requests* the Secretary-General, where appropriate, to include in his reporting to the Security Council progress on gender mainstreaming throughout peacekeeping missions and all other aspects relating to women and girls;

18. *Decides* to remain actively seized of the matter.

Bibliography

General

ABANTU for Development. The gender implications of peacekeeping and reconstruction in Africa. Report of a policy seminar, 30 -31 March 2000, Mombassa, Kenya. ABANTU Publications, May 2000.

Abdela, Lesley. After humanitarian action: democratisation; Local institutions and gender. In Kosovo and the Changing Face of Humanitarian Action. Proceedings from a conference arranged by the Collegium for Development Studies. Uppsala University, in co-operation with Globkom, 2001.

ACORD. Annual report, ERT4: Seraye Credit and Savings Scheme -Towards Sustainability? Asmara, ACORD, 1996.

Amnesty International. Pakistan: Insufficient Protection of Women. London, 2002.

Amnesty International. Broken Bodies, Shattered Minds: Torture and Ill-treatment of Women. London, 2001.

Amnesty International. Chechnya: Rape and Torture of Children in Chemokosovo 'Filtration Camps'. News Service, 056/00 AI, Index EUR 46/19/00, 2000.

Amnesty International. Respect, Protect, Fulfil - Women's Human Rights: State Responsibility for Abuses by 'Non-State Actors'. London, 2000.

Amnesty International. Sierra Leone: Rape and Other Forms of Sexual Violence Against Girls and Women. London, 2000.

Amnesty International. Afghanistan: Women in Afghanistan: Pawns in Men's Power Struggles. London, 1999.

Amnesty International. The International Criminal Court: Ensuring Justice for Women. London, 1998.

Amnesty International. Zaire: Rape, Killings and other Human Rights Violations by the Security Forces. London, 1997.

Amnesty International. Women's Rights are Human Rights: Commitments made by Governments in the Beijing Declaration and the Platform for Action. London, 1996.

Amnesty International. Sudan - Women's Human Rights: an Action Report. London, 1995.

Amnesty International. Women in Colombia: Breaking the Silence. London, 1995.

Anderlini, Sanam. Women, Peace and Security: A Policy Audit from the Beijing Platform for Action to United Nations Security Council Resolution 1325 and Beyond. London, International Alert, 2001.

Anderlini, Sanam. Women at the Peace Table: Making a Difference. New York, United Nations Development Fund for Women, 2000.

Anderson, Shelley. Women's many roles in reconciliation. People Building Peace: European Platform for Conflict Prevention and Transformation, n.d.

Arditti, Rita and M. Brinton Lykes. The disappeared children of Argentina: The work of the grandmothers of Plaza de Mayo. In Surviving Beyond Fear: Women, Children and Human Rights in Latin America. Marjorie Agosin, ed. New York, White Pine Press, 1993.

Arnvig, Eva. Women, Children and Returnees. In Peter Utting, ed. Between Hope and Insecurity: The Social Consequences of the Cambodian Peace Process. Geneva, United Nations Research Institute for Social Development, 1994.

Ashford, Mary-Wynne, and Yolanda Huet-Vaugn. The impact of war on women. In War and Public Health. Barry Levy and Victor Sidel, eds. Oxford, Oxford University Press, 1997.

Askin, Kelly Dawn. War Crimes Against Women: Prosecution in International War Crimes Tribunals. The Hague, Martinus Nijhoff Publishers,1997.

Astgeirsdottir, Kristin. Women, adolescent girls, and girl children in Kosovo: The effect of armed conflict on the lives of women. Paper presented at the UNFPA Consultative Group Meeting on the Impact of Armed Conflict on Women and Girls, Bratislava, Slovakia, 2001.

Baines, Erin. The Elusiveness of Gender-Related Change in International Organizations: Refugee Women, the United Nations High Commissioner for Refugees and the Political Economy of Gender Ph.D Dissertation. Halifax, Nova Scotia, 2000.

Bloomfield, D., and B. Reilly. Characteristics of deep-rooted conflict. In Democracy and Deep-Rooted Conflict: Options for Negotiators. P. Harris and B. Reilly, eds. Stockholm, IDEA, 1998.

Brunet, Ariane and Stephanie Rousseau. Acknowledging violations, struggling against impunity: Women's rights, human rights. In Common Grounds: Violence Against Women in War and Armed Conflict Situations. Indai Lourdes Sajor, ed. Quezon City, Asian Centre for Women's Human Rights, 1998.

Buck, Thomas, Alice L. Morton, Susan Allen Nan and Feride Zurikashvili. Profile: Georgia. In Women and Civil War: Impact, Organizations, and Action. Krishna Kumar, ed. Boulder, Lynne Rienner, 2001.

Bunster, Ximena. Surviving beyond fear: Women and torture in Latin America. In Surviving Beyond Fear: Women, Children and Human Rights in Latin America. Marjorie Agosin, ed. New York, White Pine Press, 1993.

Callamard, Agnes, Barbara Bedont, Ariane Brunet, Dyan Mazurana and Madeleine Rees. Investigating Women's Rights Violations in Armed Conflicts. London and Montreal, Amnesty International and the International Centre for Human Rights and Democratic Development, 2001.

Canadian Department of Foreign Affairs and International Trade and the United Kingdom Department for International Development. Gender and Peacekeeping online training course. Available at www.dfait-maeci.gc.ca/genderandpeacekeeping.

Canadian International Development Agency. Gender Equality and Peace-building: An Operational Framework, 2001.

Carey, Henry F. Women, peace and security: The politics of implementing gender sensitivity norms in peacekeeping. In Women and International Peacekeeping. Louise Olsson and Torunn L. Tryggestad, eds. London, Frank Cass, 2001.

Carlson, Marifran. A tragedy and a miracle: Leonor Alonso and the human cost of state terrorism in Argentina. In Surviving Beyond Fear: Women, Children and Human Rights in Latin America. Marjorie Agosin, ed. New York, White Pine Press, 1993.

Carpenter, Charli R. Surfacing children: Limitations of genocidal rape discourse. *Human Rights Quarterly* vol. 22, No. 2, 2000.

Chesterman, Simon, ed. Civilians in War. Boulder, Lynne Rienner, 2001.

Chew, Phyllis Ghim Lian. The Challenge of Unity: Women, Peace and Power. *The International Journal on World Peace* vol. 15, No. 4, December 1998.

Coalition to End the Use of Child Soldiers. Child Soldiers Global Report. London, 2001.

Cock, Jacklyn. Women and War in South Africa. London, Open Letters Press, 1993.

Cockburn, Cynthia and Dubravka Zarkov, eds. The Post-war Moment: Militaries, Masculinities and International Peacekeeping - Bosnia and the Netherlands. London, Lawrence and Wishart, 2002.

Cockburn, Cynthia, Rada Stakic-Domuz and Meliha Hubic. Women Organizing for Change: A Study of Women's Local Integrative Organizations and the Pursuit of Democracy in Bosnia-Hercegovina. Sarajevo, Medica Zenica, June 2001.

Cockburn, Cynthia. The Space Between Us: Negotiating Gender and National Identities in Conflict. London, Zed Books, 1998.

Cohen, Craig and Noah Hendler. Nta Nzu Itagira Inkigi: No Home Without Foundation: A Portrait of Child-headed Households in Rwanda. New York, Women's Commission for Refugee Women and Children, 1997.

Cohen, Roberta, and Francis M. Deng. Masses in Flight: The Global Crisis of Internal Displacement. Washington, DC, Brookings Institution, 1998.

Colson, Elizabeth. War and domestic violence. *Cultural Survival Quarterly* vol. 19, No. 1, Spring 1995.

Corner, Lorraine. Women, Men and Economics: The Gender-differentiated Impact of Macroeconomics. New York, United Nations Development Fund for Women, 1996.

Corrin, Chris. Post-conflict reconstruction and gender analysis in Kosova. *International Feminist Journal of Politics* vol. 3, No. 1, 2001.

Corrin, Chris. Gender Audit of Reconstruction Pogrammes in South Eastern Europe. Fairfax, California and New York, The Urgent Action Fund and the Women's Commission for Refugee Women and Children, June 2000.

Cukier, Wendy. Vuurwapens: Legale en illegale kanalen (Translation of Firearms: Licit/Illicit links) *Tijdschrift voor Criminologie*. E.J. Frankie, E.S. de Wijs, eds. vol. 43, No. 1, March 2001.

Cukier, Wendy , Cindy Collins and Antoine Chapdelaine. Global Trade in Small Arms: Public Health Effects and Interventions. International Physicians for the Prevention of Nuclear War and SAFER-Net, March 2001.

Cukier, Wendy, Cindy Collins and Antoine Chapdelaine. Globalization of Small Arms. Rockefeller, SID/WHO Conference on Globalization and Health, 1999.

DeGroot, Gerard J. A few good women: Gender stereotypes, the military and peacekeeping. In Women and International . Peacekeeping. Louise Olsson and Torunn L. Tryggestad, eds. London, Frank Cass, 2001.

Development and Gender Institute of Development Studies. Conflict and Development. Sussex, 1996.

De Waal, Alex. Dangerous precedents? Famine relief in Somalia 1991-1993. War and Hunger: Rethinking International Responses to Complex Emergencies. In Joanna Macrae and Anthony Zwi, eds. London, Zed Books, 1994.

De Watteville, Nathalie. Addressing Gender Issues in Demobilization and Reintegration Programs. Africa Region Working Paper Series. Washington, World Bank, 2002.

Duffield, Mark. Post modern conflict: Warlords, post-adjustment states and private protection. *Journal of Civil Wars* vol. 1, No. 1, 1998.

Duffield, Mark. Global Governance and the New Wars: The Merging of Development and Security. London, Zed Books, 2001.

El-Bushra Judy, Asha El-Karib and Angela Hadjipateras. Gender-Sensitive Programme Design and Planning in Conflict-Affected Situations. Research Report. ACORD, January 2002.

Enloe, Cynthia. Maneuvers: The International Politics of Militarizing Women's Lives. Berkeley, University of California Press, 2000.

Enloe, Cynthia. The Morning After: Sexual Politics at the End of the Cold War. Berkeley, University of California Press, 1993.

European Parliament. Report on Participation of Women in Peaceful Conflict Resolution. A5-0308/2000.

Fafo Institute for Applied Social Science and the Norwegian Institute of International Affairs. Gendering Human Security: From Marginalisation to the Integration of Women in Peace-Building Recommendations for policy and practice from the NUPI Fafo Forum on Gender Relations in Post-Conflict Transitions, 2001.

Fagen, Patricia Weiss and Sally W. Yudelman. El Salvador and Guatemala: Refugee camp and repatriation experiences. In Women and Civil War: Impact, Organizations, and Action Krishna Kumar, ed. Boulder, Lynne Rienner, 2001.

Fetherston, A. Betts. Voices from war zones: Implications for training UN peacekeepers. A Future for Peacekeeping? Edward Moxon-Browne, ed. Basingstoke, MacMillan, 1998.

Fischbach, R., and B. Herbert. Domestic violence and mental health: Correlates and conundrums within and across cultures. *Social Science Medicine* vol. 45, No. 8 , 1997.

Fitzsimmons, Tracy. Engendering a new police identity? *Peace Review* vol. 10, No. 2, 1998.

Furusawa, Kiyoko and Jean Inglis. Violence against women in East Timor under the Indonesian occupation. In Common Grounds: Violence Against Women in War and Armed Conflict Situations. Indai Lourdes Sajor, ed. Quezon City, Asian Centre for Women's Human Rights, 1998.

Gardam, Judith and Hilary Charlesworth. Protection of women in armed conflict. *Human Rights Quarterly* vol. 22, 2000.

Gardam, Judith and Michelle Jarvis. Women and armed conflict: The international response to the Beijing Platform for Action. *Columbia Human Rights Law Review* vol. 32, No. 1, Fall 2000.

Gardam, Judith G. and Michelle J. Jarvis. Women, Armed Conflict and International Law. The Hague, Kluwer Law International, 2001.

Gardam, Judith. Women and the law of armed conflict: Why the silence? *International and Comparative Law Quarterly* vol. 46 ,1997.

Gardam, Judith. Women, human rights and international humanitarian law *International Review of the Red Cross* No. 324, September 1998.

Garrard-Burnett, Virginia. Aftermath: Women and gender issues in post-conflict Guatemala; Working Paper No. 311. Centre for Development Information and Evaluation. Washington, DC, U.S. Agency for International Development, 2000.

Garrard-Burnett. Profile: Guatemala. In Women and Civil War: Impact, Organizations, and Action. Krishna Kumar ed. Boulder, Lynne Rienner, 2001.

Gasa, N. National machinery for gender equality. In Democracy and Deep-rooted Conflict: Options for Negotiators. P. Harris and B. Reilly, eds. Stockholm, IDEA, 1998.

Giles, Wenona and Jennifer Hyndman. Sites of Violence: Gender and Conflict Zones. Forthcoming.

Goldstein, Joshua S. War and Gender. Cambridge, Cambridge University Press, 2001.

Hansen, Lene. Gender, nation, rape: Bosnia and the construction of security. *International Feminist Journal of Politics* vol. 3, No. 1, 2001.

Heise, Lori, Jacqueline Pitanguy, Adrienne Germain. Violence Against Women: The Hidden Health Burden. Washington, D.C, World Bank, 1994.

Helland, Anita, Kari, Karamé, Anita Kristensen, and Inger Skjelsbæk. Women and Armed Conflict: A Study for the Norwegian Ministry of Foreign Affairs. Oslo, Norwegian Ministry of Foreign Affairs, 1999.

Hill, Felicity. Reports of panels and presentations: women and armed conflict. Building a Women's Peace Agenda. Hague Appeal for Peace, ed. New York, Gender Focus Group of the Hague Appeal for Peace, 2001.

Hoskins, Eric. Public health and the Persian Gulf war. War and Public Health. Barry Levy and Victor Sidel, eds. Oxford, Oxford University Press, 1997.

Hudson, Heidi. Mainstreaming gender in peacekeeping operations: Can Africa learn from international experience? *African Security Review* vol. 9, No. 4, 2000.

Human Rights Watch. The War Within War. Sexual Violence against Women and Girls in Eastern Congo. New York, June 2002.

Human Rights Watch. Afghanistan: Humanity Denied, Systematic Violations of Women's Rights in Afghanistan. vol. 13 No. 5, New York, October 2001.

Human Rights Watch Women's Rights Project. Kosovo: Rape as a Weapon of 'Ethnic Cleansing'. vol. 12, No. 3 (D), March 2000.

Human Rights Watch. World Report 2000. New York, 2000.

Human Rights Watch. Leave None To Tell the Story: Genocide in Rwanda. New York, 1999.

Human Rights Watch. World Report 1999. New York, 1999.

Human Rights Watch Africa and Human Rights Watch Women's Rights Project. Shattered Lives: Sexual Violence During the Rwandan Genocide and Its Aftermath. New York, 1996.

INCORE (Initiative on Conflict Resolution and Ethnicity). Men, Women, and War Conference. 1997.

InterAction. Weaving Gender in Disaster and Refugee Assistance. Washington, 1998.

International Alert. Gender and Conflict: Early Warning. London, 2002.

International Alert. Gender and Peace Support Operations: Opportunities and Challenges to Improve Practice. London, 2001.

International Alert. Implementing the United Nations Security Council Resolution on Women, Peace and Security: Integrating Gender into Early Warning Systems. Report on the First Expert Consultative Meeting, Nairobi, Kenya, 2001.

International Alert. Women, Violent Conflict and Peace-building: Global Perspectives Proceedings from an International Conference. London, 1999.

International Committee of the Red Cross. Arms Availability and the Situation of Civilians in Armed Conflict. Geneva, 1999.

International Committee of the Red Cross. Women Facing War. Geneva, 2001.

International Fellowship of Reconciliation. Women and Peacemaking: Lessons Learned from the Women's Peacemakers Program. The Netherlands, 2002.

International Fellowship of Reconciliation. Women Lead the Way to Peace. Alkmaar, Netherlands, 1999.

International Organization for Migration. Anti-Trafficking Program in Kosovo – Through Prevention, Awareness Raising, Capacity Building and Facilitation. New York, n.d.

International Organization for Migration. Victims of Trafficking in the Balkans: A study of trafficking in women and children for sexual exploitation to, through and from the Balkan region. Vienna/Geneva, 2001.

International Rescue Committee. Promoting the Rights of Children in Emergencies: A Case Study of Child and Community Participation in the IRC's Non-formal Education and Psychosocial Support Project in Ingushetia. New York, 2002 [draft].

International Save the Children Alliance. Promoting Psychosocial Well-being Among Children Affected by Armed Conflict and Displacement: Principles and Approaches. Westport, Connecticut, 1996.

Isis-WICCE. Medical Intervention Study of War Affected Gulu District, Uganda. Kampala, 2001.

Isis-WICCE. Women's Experiences of Armed Conflict in Uganda, Gulu District 1986-1999. Kampala, 2001.

Iyob, Ruth. "The Eritrean experiment: A cautious pragmatism?" Journal of Modern African Studies, vol. 35, No. 4 (1997.

Jacobs, Susie, Ruth Jacobso, and Jennifer Marchbank eds. States of Conflict: Gender, Violence and Resistance. London, Zed Books, 2000.

Julia, Maria. Revisiting a repopulated village: A step backwards in the changing status of women. International Social Work, vol. 38, 1995.

Juma, Monica Kathina. Unveiling Women as Pillars of Peace: Peace Building in Communities Fractured by Conflict in Kenya - an Interim Report. Management Development and Governance Division, Bureau for Development Policy, United Nations Development Programme, May 2000.

Karam, Azza. Women in war and peace-building: The roads traversed, the challenges ahead. International Feminist Journal of Politics vol. 3, No. 1, 2001.

Karamé, Kari H. Military women in peace operations: Experiences of the Norwegian battalion in UNIFIL 1978-98. In Women and International Peacekeeping. Louise Olsson and Torunn L. Tryggestad, eds. London, Frank Cass, 2001.

Kien, Serey Phal. The lessons of the UNTAC experience and the ongoing responsibilities of the international community for peace-building and development in Cambodia. *Pacifica Review* vol. 7, No. 2, October/November 1995.

Kosovo and the Changing Face of Humanitarian Action. Proceedings from a conference arranged by the Collegium for Development Studies, Uppsala University, in co-operation with Globkom, 2001.

Kumar, Krishna. Ed. Women and Civil War: Impact, Organizations, and Action. Boulder, Lynne Rienner, 2001.

Kumar, Krishna and Hannah Baldwin. Women's organizations in post-conflict Cambodia. In Women and Civil War: Impact, Organizations, and Action. Krishna Kumar, ed. Boulder, Lynne Rienner, 2001.

Kumar, Krishna, Hannah Baldwin and Judy Benjamin. Profile: Cambodia. In Women and Civil War: Impact, Organizations, and Action. Krishna Kumar, ed. Boulder, Lynne Rienner, 2001.

Kumar, Krishna. Civil wars, women, and gender relations: An overview. In Women and Civil War: Impact, Organizations, and Action. In Krishna Kumar, ed. Boulder, Lynne Rienner, 2001.

Kumar, Krishna. Women's and Women's Organizations in Post-Conflict Societies: The Role of International Assistance. Washington, Centre for Development Information and Evaluation, United States Agency for International Development, 2000.

Kvinna till Kvinna. Getting it Right? A Gender Approach to UNMIK Administration in Kosovo. Stockholm, 2001.

Kvinna till Kvinna. Engendering the Peace Process: A Gender Approach to Dayton - and Beyond. Stockholm, 2000.

Large, Judith. Disintegration conflicts and the restructuring of masculinity. *Gender and Development* vol. 5, No. 2, 1997.

Lautze, Sue, N. Nojumi, K. Najimi, K. and E. Stites. Coping with Crisis: A Review of Coping Strategies Throughout Afghanistan 1999 -2002. Washington D.C., U.S. Agency for International Development, 2002.

Lautze, Sue. Saving Lives and Livelihoods: The Fundamentals of a Livelihoods Strategy. Feinstein International Famine Centre, Tufts University, March 1997.

Lentin, Ronit. Gender and Catastrophe. London, Zed Books, 1997.

Littlewood, R. Military rape. *Anthropology Today* vol. 13, No. 2, 1997.

Lorentzen, Lois Ann and Jennifer Turpin, eds. The Women and War Reader. New York, New York University Press, 1998.

Lupi, Natalia. Report by the Enquiry Commission on the Behaviour of Italian Peacekeeping Troops in Somalia. *Yearbook of International Humanitarian Law* vol. 1, 1998.

Macrae, Joanna, and Anthony Zwi, eds. War and Hunger: Rethinking International Responses to Complex Emergencies. London, Zed Books, 1994.

Macrae, Joanna. Aiding Recovery? The Crisis of Aid in Chronic Political Emergencies. London, Zed Books, 2001.

Mansaray, Binta. Women against weapons: A leading role for women in disarmament. Bound to Cooperate: Conflict, Peace and People in Sierra Leone. Anatole Ayissi and Robin-Edward Poulton, eds. Geneva, United Nations Institute for Disarmament Research, December 2000.

Markus, Michael, D. Meddings, S. Ramez, and J. Gutiérrez-Fisac. Incidence of weapon injuries not related to interfactional combat in Afghanistan in 1996: Prospective cohort study. *BMJ* No. 319, 1999.

Marshall, Donna Ramsey. Women in war and peace: Grassroots peace-building. United States Institute of Peace, *Peaceworks* No. 34, 2000.

Matthews, S. Women in conflict. *Conflict Trends* vol. 4, 2000.

Mazurana, Dyan and Susan McKay. Women and Peace-building. Montreal, International Centre for Human Rights and Democratic Development, 1999.

Mazurana, Dyan, Susan McKay, Khristopher Carlson, and Janel Kasper. Girls in fighting forces: Their recruitment, participation, demobilization, and reintegration. *Peace and Conflict* vol. 8, No. 2, 2002.

McKay, Susan and Dyan Mazurana. Raising Women's Voices for Peace-building. London, International Alert, 2001.

McKay, Susan. Gender justice and reconciliation. *Women's Studies International Forum* vol. 23, No. 5, 2000.

Meddings, David, and Stephanie M. Connor. Circumstances around weapon injury in Cambodia after departure of a peacekeeping force: prospective cohort study. *BMJ* No. 319, 1999.

Meintjes, Sheila, Anu Pillay and Meredeth Turshen, eds. The Aftermath: Women in Post-conflict Transformation. London, Zed Books, 2002.

Mertus, Julie A. War's Offensive on Women: The Humanitarian Challenge in Bosnia, Kosovo, and Afghanistan. Bloomfield, Connecticut, Kumarian Press, 2000.

Mladjenovic, Lepa. Ethics of difference—Working with women survivors. In Common Grounds: Violence Against Women in War and Armed Conflict Situations. Indai Lourdes Sajor, ed. Quezon City, Asian Centre for Women's Human Rights, 1998.

Mohanty, Chandra Talpade. Cartographies of struggle: Third world women and the politics of feminism. In Third World Women and the Politics of Feminism. C.T. Mohanty, A. Russo and L. Torres, eds. Bloomington, Indiana University Press, 1991.

Morton, Alice L., Susan Allen Nan, Thomas Buck, and Feride Zurikashvili. Georgia in Transition: Women's Organizations in and Empowerment. In Women and Civil War: Impact, Organizations, and Action. Krishna Kumar, ed. Boulder, Lynne Rienner, 2001.

Moser, Caroline O.N. and Clark, Fiona C., eds. Victims, Perpetrators or Actors? Gender, Armed Conflict and Political Violence. London, Zed Books, 2001.

Moser-Puangsuwan, Yeshua. U.N. peacekeeping in Cambodia: Whose needs were met? *Pacifica Review* vol. 7, No. 2 1995.

Mrsevic, Zorica, and Donna Hughes. Violence against women in Belgrade, Serbia. *Violence Against Women* vol. 3, No. 2 April 1997.

Mudrovèiæ, Željka. Sexual and Gender-Based Violence in Post-Conflict Regions: The Bosnia and Hercegovina Case. Paper presented at UNFPA Consultative Group Meetings on the Impact of Conflict on Women and Girls, 13-15 November 2001 at Bratislava, Slovakia.

Naraghi-Anderlini, Sanam. Women's Leadership, Gender and Peace. Reflections on a Meeting at the Ford Foundation, 2001.

Naslund, E. Looking at peace through women's eyes: Gender-based discrimination in the Salvadoran peace process. *Journal of Public and International Affairs* vol. 10 1999.

Netherlands Committee on Human Rights and Vrouwenberaad Ontwikkelings-samenwerking. War and Peace: For Men Only? Report of a Public Forum, 26 January 1996, Amsterdam, the Netherlands.

Newbury, Catharine and Hannah Baldwin. Confronting the aftermath of conflict: Women's organizations in post-genocide Rwanda. In Women and Civil War: Impact, Organizations, and Action. Krishna Kumar, ed. Boulder, Lynne Rienner, 2001.

Newbury, Catharine and Hannah Baldwin. Profile: Rwanda. In Women and Civil War: Impact, Organizations, and Action. Krishna Kumar, ed. Boulder, Lynne Rienner, 2001.

NGO Working Group on Women and International Peace and Security. Security Council Resolution 1325 on Women, Peace and Security: One Year On. 2001.

Ogunsanya, Kemi and Kwezi Mngqibisa. A gender perspective for conflict management. ACORD Occasional paper No. 4, 2000.

Olsson, Louise. Gender mainstreaming in practice: The United Nations Transitional Assistance Group in Namibia. In Women and International Peacekeeping. Louise Olsson and Torunn Tryggestad, eds. London, Frank Cass Publishers, 2001.

Olsson, Louise. Gendering UN peacekeeping: Mainsteaming a gender perspective in multidimensional peacekeeping operations. Uppsala University Department of Peace and Conflict. Research Report No. 53 1999.

Physicians for Human Rights. Women's Health and Human Rights in Afghanistan: A Population-Based Assessment Boston, 2001.

Ransom, Pam. Reports of panels and presentations: women and peace-building. In Building a Women's Peace Agenda. Hague Appeal for Peace, ed. New York, Gender Focus Group of the Hague Appeal for Peace, 2001.

Raven-Roberts, Angela. Participation, citizenship and the implications of women's activism in the creation of a culture of peace. In Women and A Culture of Peace, UNESCO, 1999.

Ready, Kelley, Lynn Stephen, and Serena Cosgrove. Women's organizations in El Salvador: History, accomplishments and international support. In Women and Civil War: Impact, Organizations, and Action Krishna Kumar, ed. Boulder, Lynne Rienner, 2001.

Rooney, Eilish. Mapping gender terrain in the Northern Irish conflict. Paper delivered at the International Studies Association Annual Convention, Washington 1999.

Rosca, Ninotchka. Effects of militarism and state violence on women and children. Human Rights in the Twenty-first Century. K.E. Mahoney and P. Mahoney, eds. Netherlands, Kluwer Academic Publishers, 1993.

Ruberry, M. The effects of landmines on women in the Middle East. *Journal of Mine Action* vol. 5, No. 3, Fall 2001.

Ruecker, Kirsten. Engendering Peace-building: Case Studies from Cambodia, Rwanda and Guatemala. Report for the Peace-building and Human Security Division, Department of Foreign Affairs and International Trade, Ottawa, Canada, January 2000.

Sajor, Indai Lourdes, ed. Common Grounds: Violence Against Women in War and Armed Conflict Situations. Quezon City, Asian Centre for Women's Human Rights, 1998.

Samuel, Kumudini. Gender difference in conflict resolution: The case of Sri Lanka. In Gender, Peace and Conflict. Inger Skjelsbæk and Dan Smith. eds. London, Sage Publications, 2001.

Sharoni, Simona. Gender and the Israeli-Palestinian Conflict: The Politics of Women's Resistance. Syracuse, Syracuse University Press, 1995.

Skjelsbæk, Inger and Dan Smith. eds. Gender, Peace and Conflict. London, Sage Publications, 2001.

Skjelsbæk, Inger. Sexual violence at times of war: A new challenge for peace operations? In Women and International Peacekeeping. Louise Olsson and Torunn L. Tryggestad, eds. London, Frank Cass, 2001.

Soudiere, Marie de la. The Impact of War in the Former Yugoslavia: A Needs Assessment. Geneva, UNHCR, 1993.

Sørensen, Brigitte. Women and Post-Conflict Reconstruction: Issues and Sources. Geneva, United Nations Research Institute for Social Development and the Programme for Strategic and International Security Studies, 1998.

Stiehm, Judith Hicks. Peacekeeping and peace research: Men's and women's work. *Women and Politics* vol. 8, 1997.

Stiehm, Judith Hicks. Women, peacekeeping and peacemaking: Gender balance and mainstreaming. In Women and International Peacekeeping. Louise Olsson and Torunn L. Tryggestad, eds. London, Frank Cass, 2001.

Stiglmayer, Alexandra, ed. Mass Rape: The War Against Women in Bosnia-Herzegovina. Lincoln, University of Nebraska Press, 1994.

Swedish International Development Agency. Post-Conflict Initiatives and Equality between Women and Men: Why Are Gender Equality Issues Relevant in Post-Conflict Initiatives? December 1998.

The Women's Foreign Policy Group. The Changing Nature of Conflict: New Dimensions, New Players. Washington, DC, New Perspectives, 2001.

Thompson, Carol. Beyond civil society: Child soldiers as citizens in Mozambique. *Review of African Political Economy* vol. 80, 1999.

Toole, M., and Waldman, R.J. Refugees and displaced persons: War, hunger and public health. *Journal of the American Medical Association* vol. 270, 1993.

Tuft, Eva Irene. Integrating a gender perspective in conflict resolution: The Colombian case. In Gender, Peace and Conflict. Inger Skjelsbæk and Dan Smith, eds. London, Sage Publications, 2001.

Turshen, Meredeth and Twagiramariya, Clotilde, eds. What Women Do in Wartime: Gender and Conflict in Africa London, Zed Books, 1998.

United States Commission for Refugees. World Refugee Survey 2001. Washington, D.C., 2002.

Utting, Peter. ed. Between Hope and Insecurity: The Social Consequences of the Cambodian Peace Process. Geneva: United Nations Research Institute for Social Development, 1994.

Walsh, Martha, Women's organizations in post-conflict Bosnia and Herzegovina. In Women and Civil War: Impact, Organizations, and Action. Krishna Kumar, ed. Boulder, Lynne Rienner, 2001.

Walsh, Martha. Profile: Bosnia and Herzegovina. In Women and Civil War: Impact, Organizations, and Action. Krishna Kumar, ed. Boulder, Lynne Rienner, 2001.

Ward, Jeanne. If Not Now, When? Addressing Gender-Based Violence in Refugee, Internally Displaced, and Post-Conflict Settings: A Global Overview. New York, The Reproductive Health for Refugee Consortium, 2002.

Watanuki, Reiko. The reproductive health of Vietnamese women and chemical weapons. In Common Grounds: Violence Against Women in War and Armed Conflict Situations. Indai Lourdes Sajor, ed. Quezon City, Asian Centre for Women's Human Rights, 1998.

Watson, Carol. The Flight, Exile and Return of Chadian Refugees: A Case Study With a Special Focus on Women. Geneva, UNRISD, 1996.

Whitworth, Sandra. Gender, race and the politics of peacekeeping. In A Future for Peacekeeping? Edward Moxon-Browne. ed. Basingstoke, Macmillan, 1998.

Whitworth, Sandra. Militarized masculinities and the politics of peacekeeping: The Canadian case. In Security, Community and Emancipation. K. Booth. Ed. Boulder, Lynne Rienner, [forthcoming].

Williams, Suzanne. Report of Visit to the Refugee Camps in Macedonia. Oxfam, UK, 1999.

Women's Commission for Refugee Women and Children. Disarmament, Demobilization and Reintegration: Assessing Gaps in Policy and Protection in Sierra Leone for War-affected Children and Adolescents. New York, 2002.

Women's Commission for Refugee Women and Children. Rights, Reconstruction and Enduring Peace: Afghan Women & Children after the Taliban. December 2001.

Women's Commission for Refugee Women and Children. Refugee and Internally Displaced Women and Children in Serbia and Montenegro. New York, September 2001.

Women's Commission for Refugee Women and Children, Untapped Potential: Adolescents Affected by Armed Conflict. New York, 2000.

Women's Commission for Refugee Women and Children. Kosovo Refugees: A Humanitarian and Human Rights Emergency in Albania. New York, 1999.

Women's Commission for Refuge Women and Children. Rwanda's Women and Children: The Long Road to Reconciliation. New York, 1997.

World Bank. Integrating Gender into the World Bank's Work: A Strategy for Action. Washington, D.C., 2002.

United Nations Publications (selection)

An Agenda for Peace. New York, United Nations, 1992.

From Beijing to Beijing +5, Report of the Secretary-General, Review and appraisal of the implementation of the Beijing Platform for Action. New York, United Nations, 2001.

Guiding Principles on Internal Displacement. (E/CN.4/1998/53/Add.2.)

Human Development Report. Deepening Democracy in a Fragmented World. New York/Oxford, Oxford University Press, 2002.

Machel, Graça. The Impact of Armed Conflict on Children: A critical review of progress made and obstacles encountered in increasing protection for war-affected children UNIFEM and UNICEF, Winnipeg, Canada, 2000.

Recommendations of the Special Committee on Peacekeeping Operations and the Panel on United Nations Peace Operations. (A/55/977).

Report of the Expert of the Secretary-General, Ms. Graça Machel, Impact of Armed Conflict on Children (A/51/306).

Report of the Fourth World Conference on Women, Beijing, 4-15 September 1995 (United Nations publication, Sales No. E.96.IV.13)

Report of the Panel on United Nations Peace Operations (A/55/305-S/2000/809).

Report of the World Conference to Review and Appraise the Achievements of the United Nations Decade for Women: Equality, Development and Peace, Nairobi, 15-26 July 1985 (United Nations publication, Sales No. E.85.IV.10).

Reproductive Health in Refugee Situations: An Inter-Agency Field Manual. WHO, UNFPA, UNHCR, Geneva, 1999.

United Nations Children's Fund. Cape Town Annotated Principles and Best Practices. Adopted by the participants in the Symposium on the Prevention of Recruitment of Children into the Armed Forces and Demobilization and Social Reintegration of Child Soldiers in Africa, organized by UNICEF in cooperation with the NGO Sub-group of the NGO Working Group on the Convention on the Rights of the Child, Cape Town. 1997.

United Nations Children's Fund. The Gender Dimensions of Internal Displacement: Concept Paper and Annotated Bibliography, Office of Emergency Programs Working Paper Series

United Nations Children's Fund Eastern and Southern Africa Regional Office. Interagency Meeting on Demobilization of Child Soldiers in Active Combat, Nairobi, 2001

United Nations Department for Disarmament Affairs. Gender Perspectives on Disarmament, Briefing Notes. 2001.

United Nations Department of Peacekeeping Operations. Disarmament, Demobilization and Reintegration of Ex-combatants in a Peacekeeping Environment: Principles and Guidelines. 1999.

United Nations Department of Peacekeeping Operations, Lessons Learned Unit. Mainstreaming a Gender Perspective in Multidimensional Peace Operations. 2000.

United Nations Development Fund for Women. Women's Land and Property Rights in Situations of Conflict and Reconstruction. 2001.

United Nations Development Fund for Women. Engendering Peace: Reflections on the Peace Process of Burundi. 2000.

United Nations Development Fund for Women. Resolutions of the Multiparty Conference of the Women of Burundi for Peace. 2000.

United Nations Development Fund for Women. A Commitment to the World's Women: Perspectives on Development for Beijing and Beyond. 1995.

United Nations Division for the Advancement of Women and the Department of Economic and Social Affairs. *Women 2000: Sexual violence and armed conflict: United Nations response.* 1998.

United Nations High Commissioner for Refugees. Respect Our Rights: Partnership for Equality: Report on the Dialogue With Refugee Women, Geneva Switzerland 20-22 June 2001. Geneva, 2001.

United Nations High Commissioner for Refugees. Operational Framework for Repatriation and Reintegration Activities in Post-Conflict Situations. Geneva, 1999.

United Nations High Commissioner for Refugees. Sexual Violence Against Refugees. Geneva, 1995.

United Nations High Commissioner for Refugees. Guidelines on the Protection of Refugee Women. Geneva, 1991.

United Nations High Commissioner for Refugees and Save the Children UK.

Note for Implementing and Operational Partners on Sexual Violence and Exploitation: The Experience of Refugee Children in Guinea, Liberia and Sierra Leone. February 2002.

United Nations High Commissioner for Refugees and Save the Children-UK. Sexual Violence and Exploitation: The Experience of Refugee Children in Liberia, Guinea and Sierra Leone, January 2002, Report of UNHCR/Save-UK Assessment Mission, of 22 October to 30 November 2001.

United Nations Office of the Special Adviser on Gender Issues and Advancement of Women. Gender Mainstreaming: An Overview. New York, United Nations, 2001.

United Nations Population Fund. The Impact of Conflict on Women and Girls: A UNFPA Strategy for Gender Mainstreaming in Areas of Conflict and Reconstruction. Bratislava, Slovakia, 2001.

United Nations Research Institute for Social Development. Rebuilding War-torn Societies: Report of the Working Seminar at Cartigny, Geneva 29 November -1 December 1993. Geneva, 1993.